Let hope arise!

TABLE OF CONTENTS

Printed in South Korea.

For permission requests and information, write to
Christina Showalter at PO Box 132 Linville, Virginia 22834.

ISBN: 978-0-578-64627-5

Photographs by Christina Showalter, unless otherwise credited

Written by Christina Showalter

Interviews conducted by Aaron and Christina Showalter

Edited by Melodie Davis

Proofreading by Carolyn Stone and Kent Martin

Design and layout by Holly Harrell

Cover photographs by Christina Showalter

ENDORSEMENTS

It has been my pleasure and privilege to work with Betel in the North East of England. It has been amazing to see the transformation in the lives of hundreds of men and women who have come and found a home, a community to belong to and meaningful employment.

Betel helps them move from lives of despair with addictions to finding hope and a positive future, from dependency to lives of hope and self-sufficiency. Betel is a unique ministry providing the very best recovery to the most needy in our communities.

Congratulations to Kent, Mary Alice and the whole team. You are seeing miracles every day.

—Sir Peter Vardy
Chairman, Vardy Foundation

This book leaves you with such a warm glow and a deep inner sense of "This is what it's all about!" These photos and stories are just a few of the thousands of lives utterly transformed through the power of the loving Christian communities found in all the Betel centers around the world. No statistics, messages, or even preaching could convey more that these simple photos and stories: the light and joy in these faces says it all! Jesus saves, heals and delivers, and releases broken people into their destiny.

—Gordon Hickson

I have known of the work of Betel from its early days. Kent and Mary Alice Martin were close friends even before they came to the UK to set up Betel. We have related with them strongly both personally and from within Ground Level, a network of 80 plus churches in the U.K. In fact we have the Rising Cafe as part of our church in Lincoln which is run by their men and women. This has given us firsthand knowledge of the wonderful world that is Betel. The stories recorded in this book are remarkable. I have heard many of these transformation stories through the years. However I have not just heard the stories, I have witnessed the power and reality of living testimonies of totally transformed lives. This book now gives us all an opportunity to recognize that God is still performing miracles today. He still takes hold of ordinary broken people, some who have tried many times to break free and makes them special, liberated and successful children of God. May these stories stimulate your faith and inspire you to wholeheartedly follow Jesus.

—Stuart Bell BEM,
Senior Pastor Alive Church Lincoln,
UK & Team Leader-Ground Level Network

The redemption of lives through Christ at Betel is palpable and inspiring. Christina has captured the miracle of new life in Christ through the stories and pictures of wonderfully reborn men and women. This book will give you a taste of what living in Christian community at Betel is like as lives are transformed from death to new life.

—Merle Shank

My favorite thing about this book is simple; it glorifies God. Like all these amazing people in the book, I'm also a former slave to addiction whose life had become unmanageable. God took me to Betel to set me apart and put some much needed structure in my life. I became a true man while at Betel, God freed me to exuberantly experience the joyous reality of his presence. And maybe the most astonishing realization I received from it, is that God is so great and so mighty. Christina didn't choose just one person to write about, she included many stories and I love that because God requires all of us, our whole heart, not half.

—Nick Stewart

Christina has wonderfully compiled story after story of shattered, hopeless lives redeemed by the power and love of Jesus Christ. The stories are so encouraging and faith building and even though many of us were never quite in the same situations, it clearly reminds us of what Jesus did in our lives and continues to do for all who will surrender to Him.

—Dick Blackwell

This is a book that will make you cry and fill you with hope! The stories, along with the photography, paint such a vivid picture of change that you are left with a deep certainty that Jesus is able to utterly transform lives. With personal stories, great illustrations, and practical truths this book will stir your passion for Jesus and heart for the broken.

—Rachel Hickson, Heartcry for Change

The stories of the men and women at Betel will ignite hope and inspire faith. Each bears witness to the incredible kindness of our Heavenly Father and His endless pursuit to restore our broken lives. Each photograph captures a miracle of new life only made possible by an eternally good God.

—Katherine Johnson

DEDICATION

This book is dedicated to all who have been touched by addiction of any kind. May you find hope between these pages. When you read the stories and see the faces of people who have found themselves in so many different kinds of complete brokenness, which has been followed by such real and thorough restoration and beauty—our desire is that you would see light. Let hope rise up within you! Let hope build from the deepest part of your core. There is hope! Now is the time to joyfully anticipate the good that is coming.

PREFACE

Through my journey of revelation of God's goodness, doors were opened for me to fulfill a dream I had for over ten years. As a professional photographer, I had dreamed of publishing a book. More specifically, I felt God leading me with a detailed vision for a book. During a church worship service I suddenly saw in my mind's eye this very book you are holding!

Through this photo essay book containing portraits and stories of lives that have been restored from addiction and homelessness, I hope to inspire ordinary people and bring hope to the hopeless and to their families and friends. God's goodness can feel elusive and I believe this is one way to put a face on His goodness.

I traveled to the United Kingdom with my family and we spent four weeks journeying to various Betel UK centers, interviewing and photographing the people of Betel. The people you will read about in this book have gone through the Betel's recovery residences and most are now in various forms and levels of leadership within Betel.

One thing that struck me as we spent time with the men and women at each Betel center was each one of these people was so incredibly beautiful and ordinary at the same time. So often it is easy to place people who are struggling with addiction into an unfavorable category and pass judgment but we must remember they have dreams and desires and value like everyone else. We all have unique ways of coping with the things we experience in life. We all have pain and unresolved issues that need healing. Sometimes the way we deal with these issues happens in socially unacceptable and destructive ways. But when it comes down to the root, we aren't so different from each other. My hope is that as you read and see the faces behind the stories, you will see how alike we all are. And compassion will be stirred towards those who feel like they have no way out of their pain and suffering.

To quote Sam, one of the Betel directors, "To see totally insecure, 'good for nothing', lost, broken, deceitful, dishonest people restored—not just as healthy people but to see them released into their gifting—is amazing. To see them lead competitive, cutting edge businesses that compete in the highest standard markets while maintaining fantastic reputations is astounding." This is inspiring to those of us creating this book as well, and we hope that it will equally spur you to action as you read about the restoration of people's lives and the goodness of God.

INTRODUCTION

For many years I misjudged God. I didn't believe He was actually good and had my best interests in mind. As I began to purposely seek out the truth of his goodness, He began to uncover the misunderstanding I held concerning who He really was. This began a journey of finding out who I am in light of His goodness. That terrible dread of being punished no longer had a grip on me; instead I became filled with hope and began to dream of a future filled with hope and expectation.

In this book, I'm sharing stories that show it is not only possible to be free from addiction, but it's thinkable to flourish as well—and help others attain freedom. Through supporting Betel UK for many years I've seen many success stories of freedom from addictions. After interviewing over fifty people who have experienced varied levels of success and freedom from addiction I've seen the proven results that through community and Jesus it is possible to heal and move forward.

There are so many people hurting and without hope in our world. They feel stuck and can see no way out. The people around them give up and abandon them because they too have lost hope. I feel passionate about spreading hope and I believe these people have a deep purpose and value because they are all created in the image of a great God.

In the following pages you will meet men and women who found themselves in terrible situations where they hit rock bottom. You'll experience compassion for these people, for yourself and for those you know who have similar struggles. As this compassion and empathy rise, you'll notice hope rising as well. Hope is the first step in taking action, either to help yourself or someone else.

Consider Sarah, who grew up in rejection. She turned to the streets at thirteen and literally never knew anything else. Through the Betel community she has been shown there are other ways to live, that prostitution wasn't her only option. The hope she has now is liberating! Ethel, being very successful in the academic world, thought her only purpose was to keep climbing the ladder and coping with the stress through alcohol. Now she uses her skills to help others find true success and freedom.

This book will show you all people are valuable and can have hope for restoration. As you read these stories you will ache and soar at the same time. You will feel a sense of hope. Reading this book will inspire you to reach out now. Read about how leaving the pursuit of fame on London's West End theater district has brought relief and peace to Richard or how Jan has finally found peace and joy after being cheated on, walking through a debilitating disease and conquering alcoholism. Or how Peter went from sleeping in a dumpster to leading a center for men and women recovering from the same things he used to be drowning in.

Read on to see broken, addicted outcasts find hope through Jesus and community in *Escaping Addiction: Portraits of Hope and Restoration.*

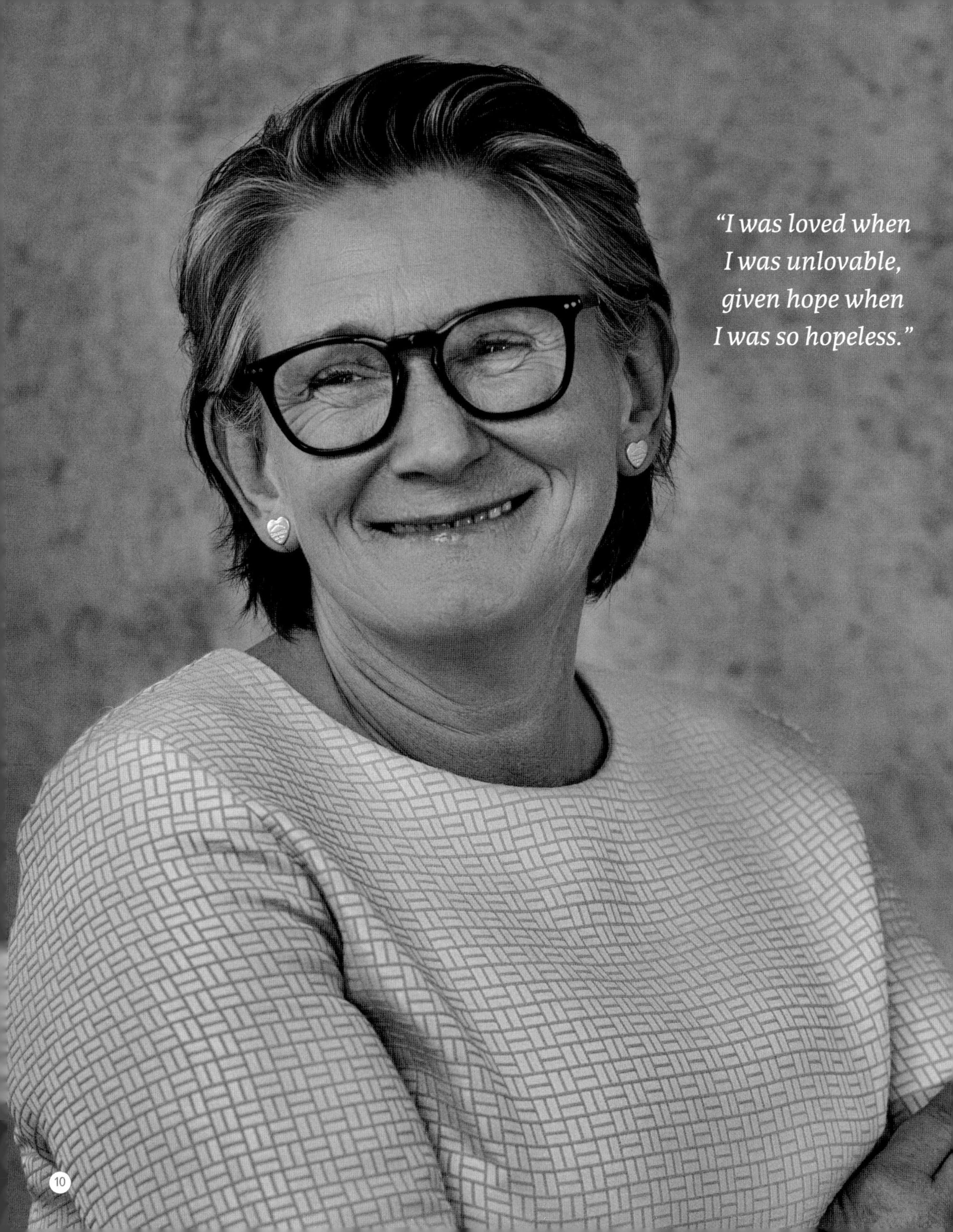
*“I was loved when
I was unlovable,
given hope when
I was so hopeless.”*

TANYA

Blackpool

"My heart was so broken. The shame and guilt of everything I had done, and all that had been done to me in my years of addiction, was great." Tanya even lost the most important thing in her life: her precious son, George. She just wanted to die.

For almost 25 years, Tanya had been a functional addict, which means she held a job and lived a seemingly normal life. In addition to years of taking LSD, magic mushrooms, and alcohol, Tanya also became addicted to crack and heroin. Her father took her to various help or rehab centers looking for solutions. They all turned her away because she was addicted to so many different substances as well as suffering mental health issues as a result from such massive drug usage. As a last resort, her dad took her to a church. Here they gave her a flyer from Betel—the only place that was willing to help her.

But Tanya didn't want help, she just wanted to die. With three bags full of 2-liter bottles of cheap alcohol cider and pockets full of drugs that she got from prostituting herself the night before, she walked to a multi-story block of flats with the intent to jump from the top.

Walking to the flats she called out to God, "If anyone is up there, please help me!" Shortly after this cry she saw a man approaching her carrying two knives. She blurted out, "Do me a favor mate, I'm not being funny, I just want to die." Little did she know that this man, Jason, was heaven sent.

Jason had been sitting in his home in the high-rise having tea when he felt prompted to look out the window. He saw Tanya sitting below and sensed he needed to help her. He took two knives from his kitchen in order to protect her, if need be, and went down to check on her.

Tanya was holding the Betel flyer and Jason happened to know the people in the photos because he had been at Betel himself for three years. He told her, "I'm here to tell you God wants you to go there." He took her home with the intent to help her get into Betel soon.

But Tanya still didn't want help, so she tried to slit one wrist, only to find that it was too painful. After binding up the wounds, she took "enough heroin to kill a donkey," only to wake up the next morning. So she upped the dosage and injected again. Once again she woke up instead of dying.

Five days later she was in Betel. Her new friends stayed by her side for three weeks straight, carrying her when she couldn't walk, and nursing her back to health. The love of Jesus came to her through these women. She told me, "I was loved when I was unlovable, given hope when I was so hopeless."

Now it is difficult to believe that these stories of her past life are true. Tanya is so amazingly full of life and joy. Her eyes crinkle in a constant smile. Her healing is so thorough and genuine. She not only has conquered her addictions but she and her husband, Jimmy, also lead a large Betel center bringing hope and restoration to many, many others.

JIMMY

Liverpool

Jimmy had dreams and aspirations plus a great academic record to go with them. The prestigious school that he worked so hard to get into had quickly turned into a nightmare for him and his friend who also was accepted. It was a fight just to survive. His friend left school and never returned after being thrown off a balcony by classmates, breaking both his arms and legs. At 13 years old, Jimmy followed suit after his hand was stabbed in a fight and badly injured.

His teen years passed working for his dad. Eventually he began hanging around with older men who led him to the party scene and drugs. Dabbling with drugs soon turned into an all-consuming addiction. Jimmy told me, "Work wasn't paying, so I started to do a lot of crime, from burglaries to robberies, drug dealing and anything else that a drug lifestyle brings." Heroin was so easy to get and it began to take over his life. But it wasn't until he added cocaine to his long list of drugs that he hit rock bottom. Things got so bad, Jimmy's girlfriend of 17 years left him, taking their son with whom he was very close. The police came and kicked Jimmy out of the house as well. At the age of 35 he was living on the streets, very ill and weighing only eight stone (112 pounds or 50 kilos).

When I asked Jimmy about choosing Betel, he told me, "I never came to Betel to become a Christian, I came because I had enough of being a drug addict. I was so full of shame and I wanted James [his son] to have a dad. That is what drove me more than anything." In spite of the addiction, Jimmy had spent a lot of time with his young son. Entering Betel meant he was separated from James which was very painful for both. Eventually, his son was able to visit and they were able to rebuild their relationship.

"I totally see God's hand in my life...I have seen His goodness guiding me to Betel. He brought me up, literally, from the gutter, and today God has blessed my life with more than I could ever want: not materially, but with love and joy. He continually opens my eyes to see Him in the small things of life."

Jimmy and his wife, Tanya, work as pastors in the Betel community, now leading Betel's newly opened work in Motherwell, just outside of Glasgow, Scotland. The joy they possess is evident and infectious as they establish a culture of hope and restoration for recovering men and women.

"I never came to Betel to become a Christian, I came because I had enough of being a drug addict."

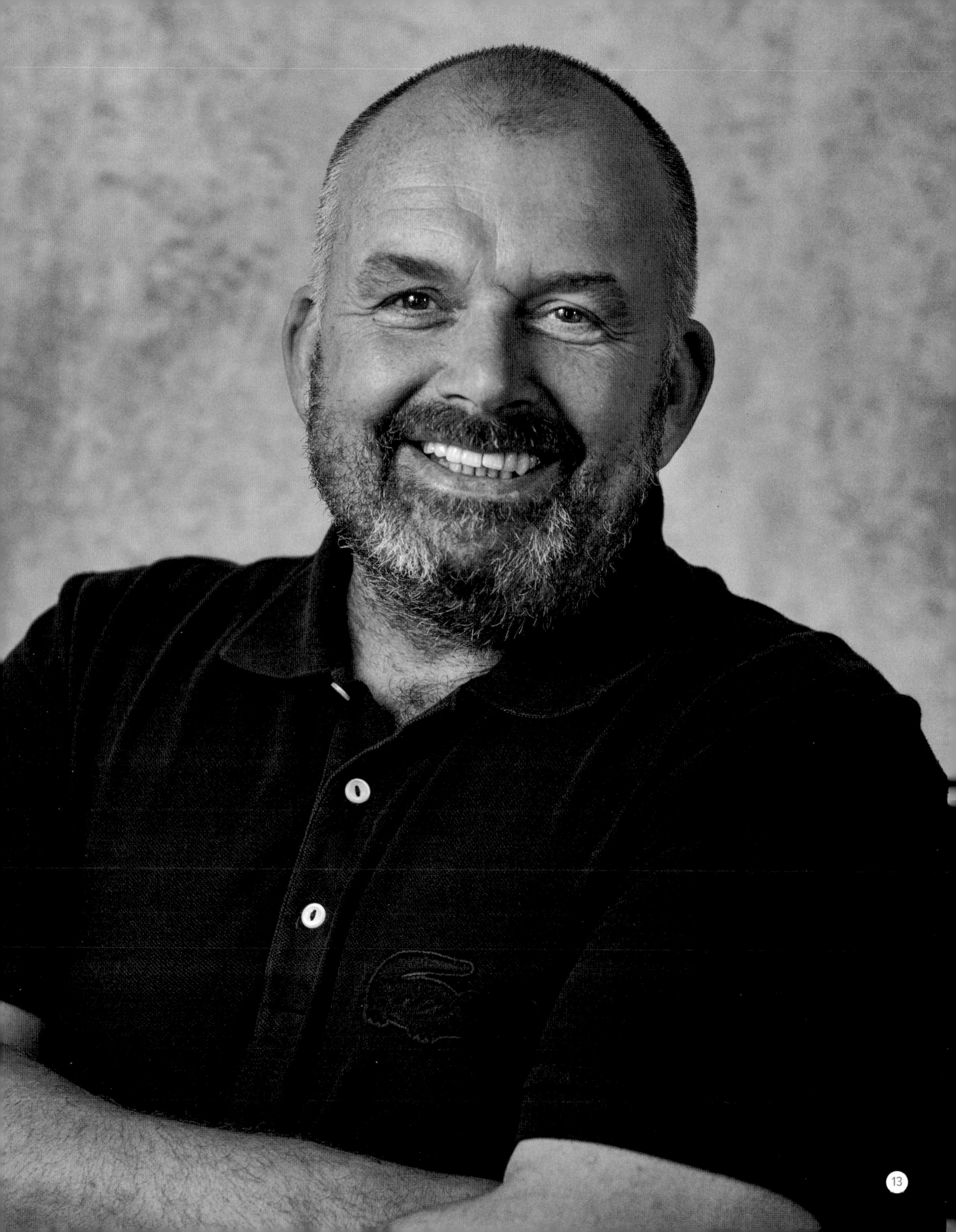

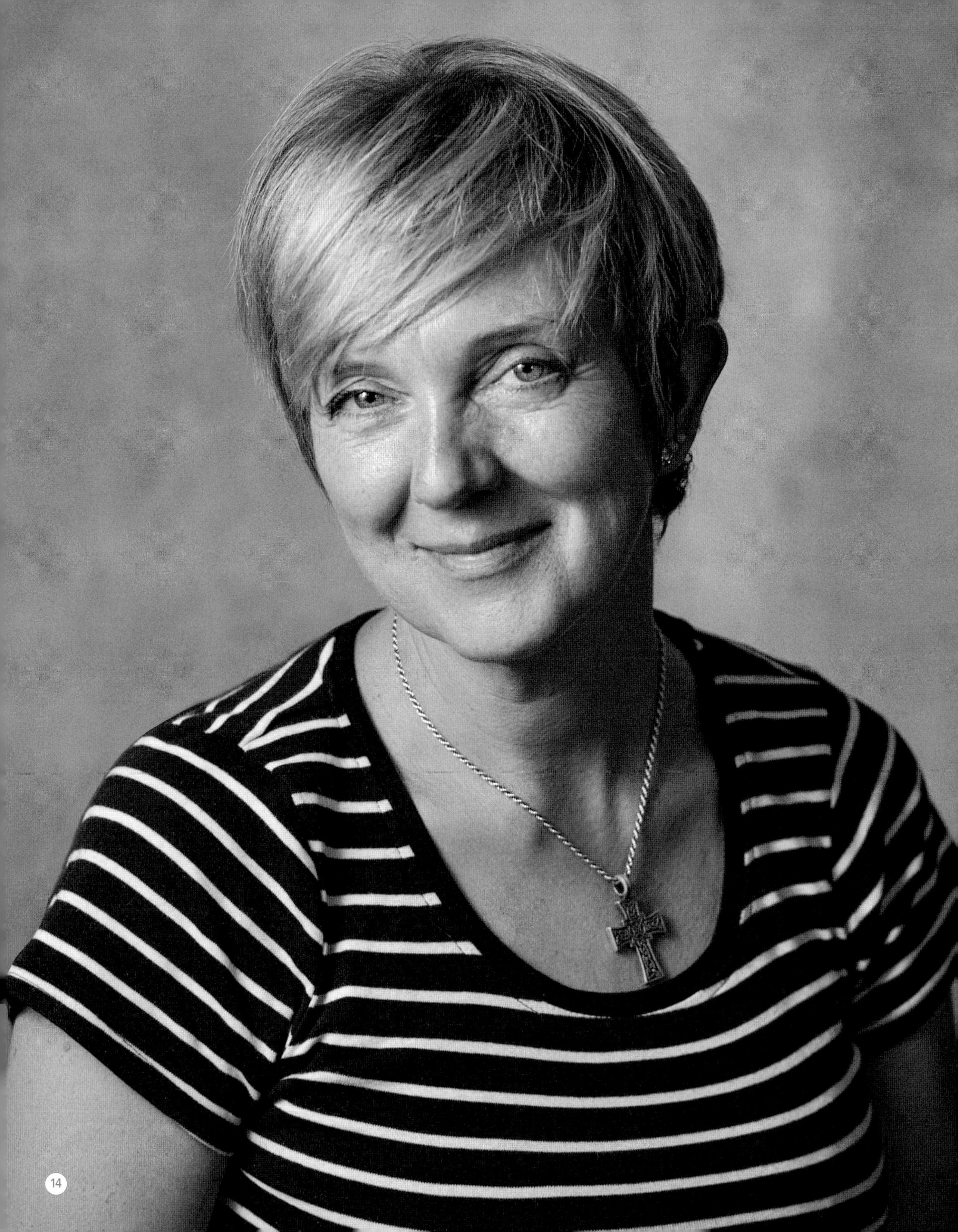

AMANDA

Birmingham

Rejecting God when she went to university and embracing a permissive lifestyle, Amanda's life was full of alcohol and pain. In spite of the excessive drinking, Amanda got married and became very successful in her career, often even traveling abroad. Amanda's heart broke after she and her husband decided to terminate her first pregnancy. After the loss of the baby, her drinking increased rapidly. Later, they did go on to have three beautiful daughters.

However, resentment regarding the abortion grew in her heart over time and caused Amanda to be quite unstable. She twice attempted suicide during her lowest times. The combination of it all was too much for their marriage and resulted in divorce. Another relationship, after her first marriage, ended the same way. Her life kept spinning out of control until her daughters were taken from her. She lost her job and home.

All this time Amanda had a heart to help other desperate people. She was hiding her own addiction in plain sight by helping others with addictions through her church. Amanda told me, "Everyone's brokenness looks different." A woman at the church saw her brokenness though, and encouraged her to go to Betel. Amanda entered 24 hours later. She told me, "God was waiting for me when I walked through the door."

Amanda says, "It is easier to see God's goodness when we look back." Her relationships with her daughters are better than ever now. As she waited on God's restoration of these relationships, she realized that "Jesus really does listen and care and love. He is working in their lives too. It is far, far better. He shows his love – it's visible and tangible." God came through in a massive way in Amanda's life.

"I used to just exist. I know now what living life in God's abundance means. I have a level of joy and peace that is beyond my understanding. And my health improves day by day. I feel fitter now than I have for 30 years! He is my life giver, my Savior, my best friend. I cannot and will not do life without Him. The dreams of my childhood are now being realized."

"I never thought I would get so low, stealing from my kids and other people. I was prostituting myself for no reason other than to have someone buy me a drink."

JASON

Bermuda

Jason never quite felt loved or accepted, and as a result he started smoking marijuana at a young age. This got him in trouble at school and with the police. He got involved in gang activity and dealing drugs. At 16 he first tried heroin and said, "I thought I found the answer to all my problems but what I didn't realize was it was the acceleration of all my problems." The cycle of prison, rehab and probation began and continued for nine years.

Sandra, a local woman who ran a rehab and drug counseling service, spent time with Jason through the years. She finally told him he needed to get off the island of Bermuda and go to a place in the UK. With the help of this community, Jason was able to stay clean for almost 11 months. However, Jason then left Betel because he felt he was ready to go back home.

After being home two weeks, Jason was outside on his mom's porch and thinking deep down that he had made the wrong move leaving Betel. "I remember my mom coming out and saying that I looked deep in thought. I told her I think I shouldn't have left England." She told me, 'If you feel that way, go back.'" Jason chalked those feelings up to missing the friends he had made in those months and it wasn't worth acting on.

Two weeks later, without any plan he got off the bus and went straight to a dealer's house. "My heart was still in a broken and wounded place and it needed something to heal it." Back on drugs, Jason's parents were crushed and he ended up back on the streets as well as in trouble with the police again. But, following conversations with Sandra and his mom, he made his way back to England. He had a sense that he needed to go back but he felt so hopeless. He couldn't figure out what Betel could possibly do for him.

Back in the UK, after an outburst of anger, his eyes were opened to his real need. "I wasn't using, wasn't with the same old friends or in the same old place but I was still the same old person." This was when he realized he needed to get to the root cause of his behavior. His quest to pursue Christianity began. Once he accepted Jesus into his life he truly began to be thoroughly changed for the better. His relationship with his family was restored and deep hurts actually began to heal.

Years later in 2016, Jason had the opportunity to taste and see God's love in a new dimension. Five weeks before his wedding to Trish, his father was diagnosed with cancer. Two weeks before the wedding they flew home to be with his dad when he passed away. It was such an emotional roller coaster that could have ruined their wedding and honeymoon. "Through that sorrow, I could have been absolutely crushed. But the sense of God's love was so intense that I felt safe to be that vulnerable, that weak." God's love proved powerful to Jason as he experienced enormous amounts of drastically different emotions, and was able to handle them in a healthy way.

Today Jason and Trish are both ordained pastors at Betel. Jason supervises Betel Birmingham, including all the finances, and leads many people from multiple locations. He also regularly teaches and preaches. Together they are changing lives and bringing innovation to Betel Birmingham.

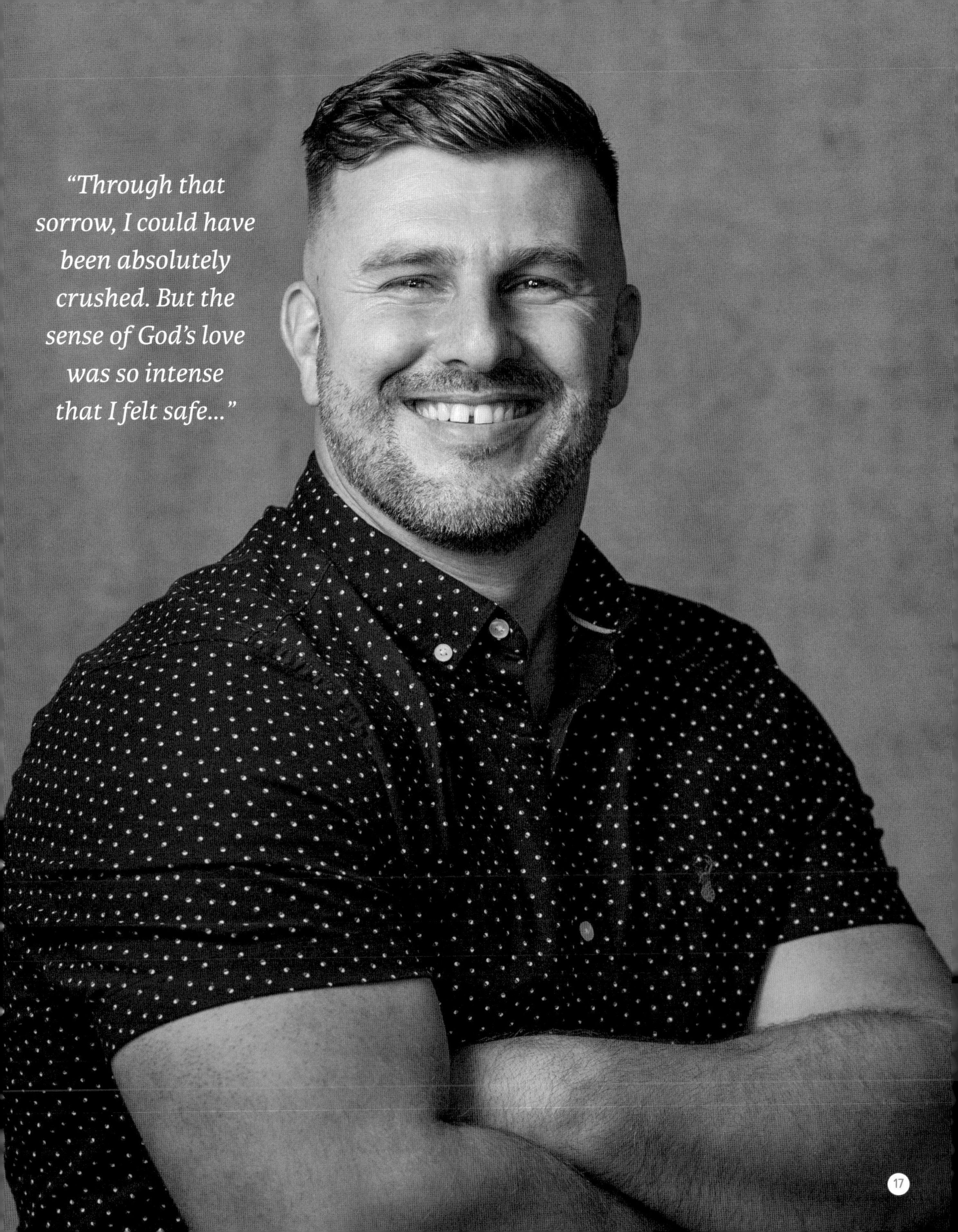

“Through that sorrow, I could have been absolutely crushed. But the sense of God’s love was so intense that I felt safe...”

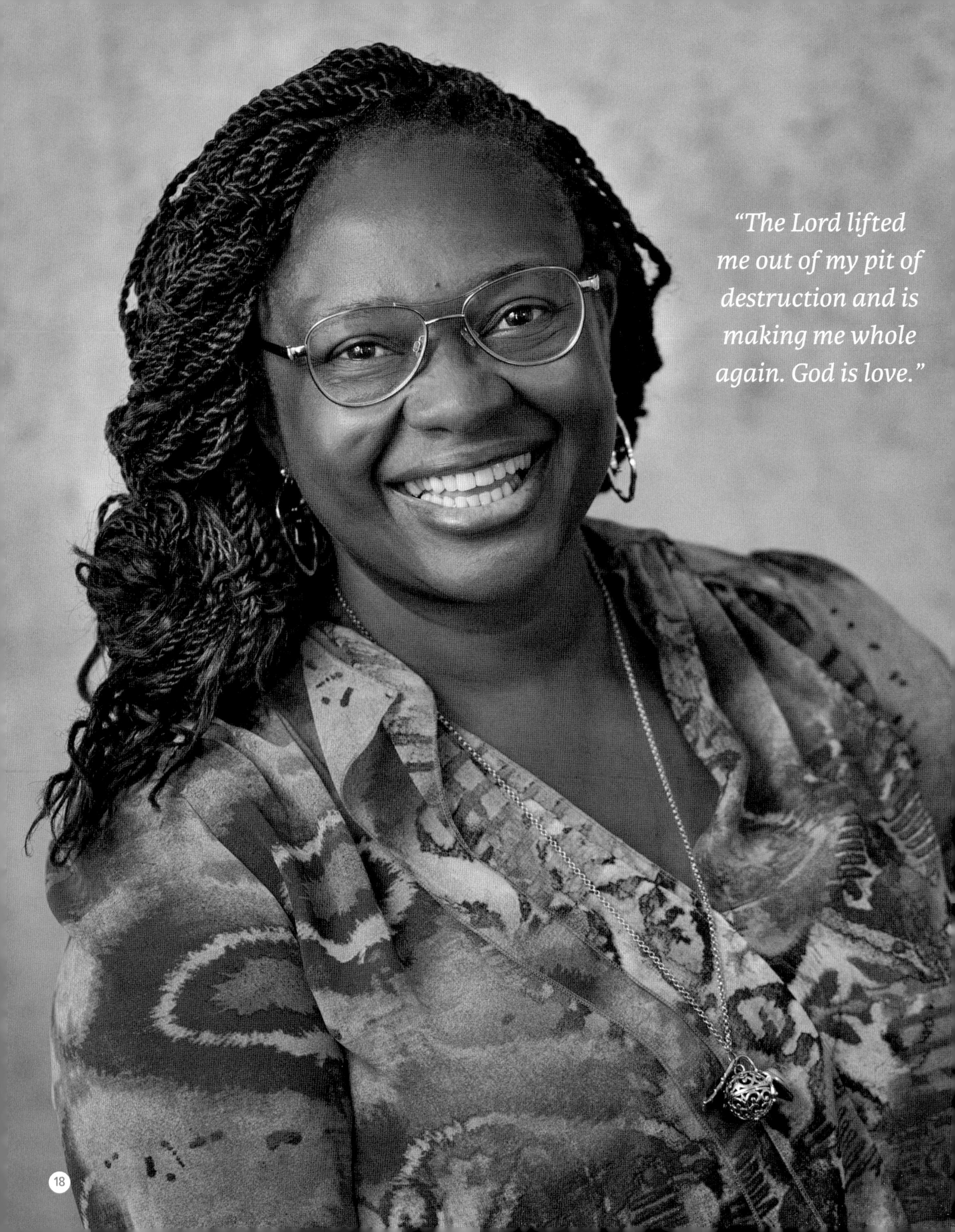
"The Lord lifted
me out of my pit of
destruction and is
making me whole
again. God is love."

ETHEL

Zimbabwe, Africa

At the age of ten, Ethel suddenly lost her mother to a brain hemorrhage. Recurring nightmares began to haunt her. Fears started creeping in about death which ended up causing massive destruction throughout her life. During this time Ethel also took on the role of running the household. She quickly became burdened by those responsibilities, coupled with juggling school and friends, and trying to fit in. All through school she was very sensitive to being different and struggled greatly with acceptance, guilt and working to please people. At the age of 14, she began drinking alcohol at teen clubs.

Despite the inner torment, Ethel became highly successful in her career in the academic world after moving to the UK for further education. Along with her ambitious husband and two children, she led a comfortable life. Then her father died when she was 30. Five years later her sister died. Ethel told us, "The 'pressure cooker' burst open. All the feelings I had been suppressing over the years came out: rage, anger, isolation, a sense of injustice, loneliness, confusion, and feeling unworthy and unloved. I turned to the bottle. Alcohol became a way of socializing, a way of coping and a way of numbing the pain day by day. I didn't want to be alive."

Ethel increasingly chose drink over everything else in her life, constantly living in an alcohol-induced oblivion. She tried every possible solution to her problems but nothing seemed to fill her emptiness. "I became a law unto myself, proud, bitter, no self-control, lacking in respect, no sense of right and wrong. I only went to church in as much as it made me self-righteous. The lifestyle I was living was one of immorality on every level."

When her brother died just four years after her sister, fear of death once again haunted her. She was convinced that her last remaining sister would be next, as well as her children. The fears became so severe that dreams of hellish torment took over her sleep once again. Alcohol became an escape from it all. Anger at God grew more intense as well. Ethel had grown up with a lot of religion, even attending several services a week. But a relationship with God was nonexistent because she was so afraid of exposing the pain buried deep within. Excess alcohol consumption, hospital admissions, and suicide attempts became her life.

This is the place where Jesus tangibly stepped in. Just three months after entering Betel, a man gifted in prophecy from God but not privy to any of her story declared Ethel's story to her. He went all the way back as far as her great grandparents in Africa. He told details of her nightmares and thoughts she never uttered aloud. She was astounded. He then told her of the freedom that she would have because of the love of Jesus. Ethel said, "On that day, curses were broken, demonic oppression was stopped, and physical healing was delivered." The hellish nightmares stopped, never to come back and restoration began in all areas of her life.

"The Lord lifted me out of my pit of destruction and is making me whole again. God is love. My biological and spiritual family know this God who is love. My desire is to see more people get to know Him and experience this love—never looking at our old lives, but holding onto His promises."

GLEN

Gloucester

"What had started as a giggle over a joint with friends, turned into a nightmare of heroin and crack addiction. The giggle launched a serious risk to my life."

Being labeled a "problem child" from early on, Glen remembers always pushing boundaries and constantly being in trouble at school. At 13, Glen came home from school to find a stranger in his home. His mom, wanting the best for her son but not knowing how to help him, had arranged for the local authority to take him into foster care. He bounced from home to home and finally was kicked out of school for good at 16. From this, Glen chose more rebellion and anger and continued with his reckless lifestyle.

During this time Glen discovered that the man he always thought was his biological father, was not. He learned that the couple he thought were his grandparents were in fact kind people who had taken in his homeless mother when she was pregnant with him and were not biologically related to him at all. Glen was thrown into more confusion than ever. It destroyed him even more. In his brokenness, he lashed out at his mother. Not understanding the pain and hardship she had endured, he unloaded his misery on her.

He and his friends spent their time smoking, inhaling solvents, and experimenting with other products, not realizing the dark and dangerous world this led to. Drugs, and all the madness that comes with them, were normal to everyone around Glen. At the age of 18 he received his first prison sentence. He ended up spending much of the next 20 years in and out of prison. "I found myself rapidly declining in health, hope, and life in general."

Glen eventually lived in a derelict building, shooting up in one room and using a side room as a toilet. At this same time, Glen's best friend, who was well off with a car and several houses and a family, often joined him on weekends for drug binges. One weekend after taking too much cocaine and ecstasy his friend suddenly died. Glen was the one who found him. The trauma threw him into another addiction, alcoholism.

One day while wandering around Gloucester he stopped in at a cathedral he frequented. He had gone through the motions of giving his heart to Jesus before, but he couldn't break free from the pull of addictions. He could see three options for where his life could head: die on the streets, go to prison again for doing something very wrong, or pursue help from Jesus. "I needed serious rescue. In my mind my life had come to an end."

Now many years later he shares, "Not only did God rescue me from death but (He) also called me to a place where He could heal my broken heart and give me purpose and hope of a bright future." After spending almost 20 years in prison he now goes into the prisons to share the hope of Jesus with the prisoners. Glen uses his talents managing a shop and leading worship at Betel. He has found a place where his identity in Christ is affirmed every day. This spills over to encourage others as he helps them find out who they were created to be.

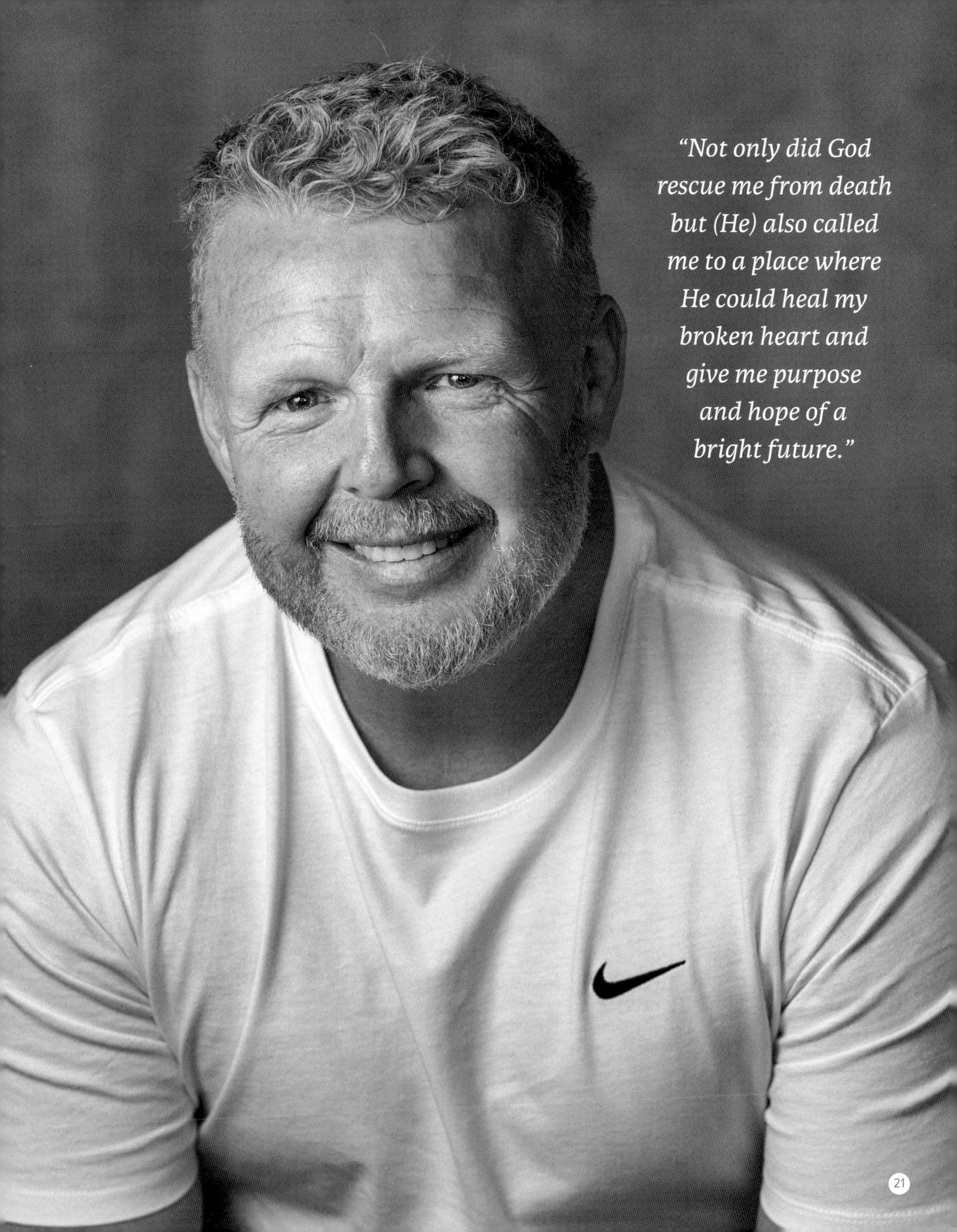

"Not only did God rescue me from death but (He) also called me to a place where He could heal my broken heart and give me purpose and hope of a bright future."

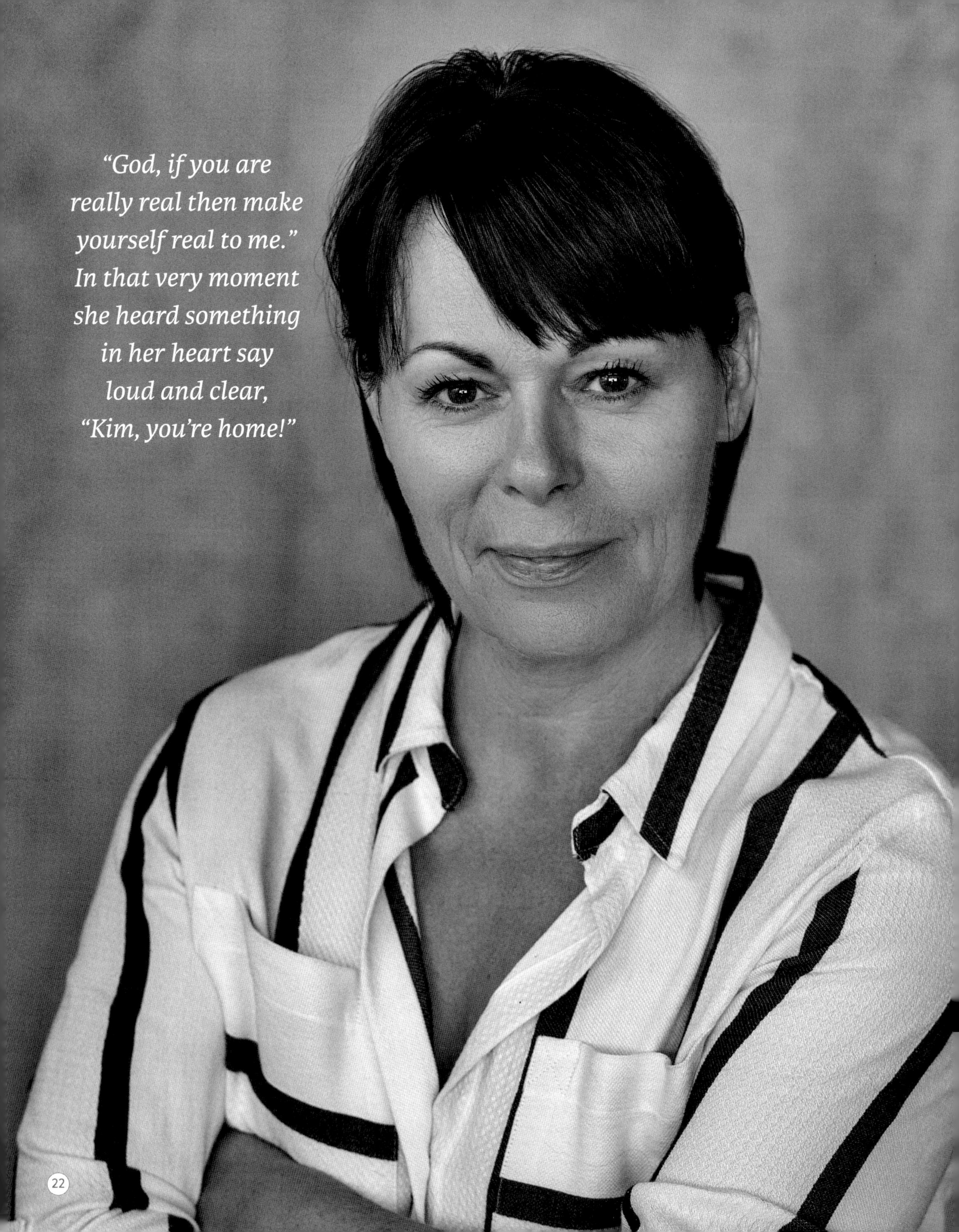
"God, if you are
really real then make
yourself real to me."
In that very moment
she heard something
in her heart say
loud and clear,
"Kim, you're home!"

KIM

Stoke

Kim's parents didn't love each other. In fact, her mum hated her dad. Since she was quite close to her dad she was rejected even more by her mother. Her mum, drunk and lying in bed with Kim, told her, "Kim, you know I love you, right?" Kim answered, "Yeah, I know." Her mother followed with, "But I'll always love Joy (one of her older sisters) a little bit more." Ultimately, her mum always rejected her. Kim said, "I always felt like I didn't belong."

After her father went to prison for abusing her older sister, her mum continued running off to parties, leaving the four girls to fend for themselves for weeks at a time. Social services got involved and put the girls into the UK foster care system. It was hard at times in the homes where they were placed. Kim recalls, "I never felt loved or really cared for. I'd run off many times just trying to find my mum, and I would be brought back and have my clothes taken away from me after school as punishment so I could not run off again."

As a teenager, Kim fell in love with Paul. They partied together for five years. Then he told her he didn't want to see her until she lost the weight she had gained from all the drugs they were using. Desperate to fit in and get him back she found someone to put speed in a needle and inject it directly into her vein. She rapidly lost the weight but not only did Paul reject her, he ended up stabbing her in the back with a Stanley blade, for which he went to prison.

By this time the speed habit had taken over and now she needed a way to come down. Thus, she began taking heroin with Andy, her new boyfriend. Eleven years and two children later, Kim was totally broken and with more than 100 criminal convictions. She said, "I did everything I said I wouldn't do to feed my habit. I was a prolific shoplifter, stole from anybody who would let me in their house, and was a prostitute for many years because I saw no way out. I went to prison so many times it became my second home. I ended up liking it there." She had no hope of ever being free from drugs. She saw everyone around her dying.

In an attempt to hide from some people who had it in for her, Kim ran to Betel for escape. This is where she found hope for the first time in her life. Two months after entering she sat on her bed crying, "God, if you are really real then make yourself real to me." In that very moment she heard something in her heart say loud and clear, "Kim, you're home!" These were the words that she most wanted to hear. No one else knew of her heart's desire to belong. Her journey of healing began at that moment.

Years later, after her sister died of a drug overdose, Kim's mother visited her for the very first time in thirteen years. Her words were so full of restoration saying, "Kim, I'm so proud of you and what you have done." Her mother died a short time later.

Today, Kim is married with two young girls, and is co-leading the women's work at Betel Birmingham. She is using her gifts and talents to bring health and healing to others.

RICHARD

Oxford

"I remember waking up in hospital, not the first or second time but the third time, from trying to commit suicide. I remember as if it was yesterday, all the wires over me, and that constant beep, beep, beep. Voices everywhere, my eyes barely opening, and then the doctor walking in saying, 'Richard, you're extremely lucky to be alive.' The words were like a slap in the face."

Since Richard was a child he always wanted to be a star! When he got older he lived his life like a theater production: it was all about Richard. He got a full scholarship to Urdang Academy and left for London at 18 years of age. By his second year, his priority switched from his studies to cocaine, other drugs and alcohol. "I never had contentment in my life. I was always putting on masks and struggling with my identity."

If society had looked in on Richard's life in London they would have said he had it all. But behind the appearances, the extravagant clothing, and the big personality, he felt lost. He said, "I was screaming out. I just didn't know how to communicate it to people, so I'd either be suicidal or do stupid things that I knew weren't right or good for me. I'd end up in really dark places."

"I really thought I had an alcohol and drug addiction. I was wrong, that was just the surface. From a young age I lived a certain lifestyle, chasing acceptance. My issue was my identity. I was completely baffled and confused as to who I was." After many dating relationships with women, Richard was having intimate relationships with men. "Even then I wasn't happy with my decision. I just thought, 'If I feel this, it must be true.'"

"One weekend I got very drunk, I woke up the next morning, eyes barely opening, sweat dripping down my face and constant shaking. My eyes opened even more and all I saw was a liter of gin, a bottle of cider, and two empty wine bottles. My heart felt as if it was going to come out of my chest. From that moment I thought, 'This is it; I'm changing my life.' I was calling out to the almighty God, in complete desperation. I grabbed my iPad and researched 'free rehab.' Betel came up and all I cared about was that it was free."

Richard's true desire was to be authentic and not just pretend or repress anything. No one told him what he had to "be" at Betel, he only felt love. He explained that "God came straight into me, he has taken everything and rinsed it out and said to me, '*This* is who you are meant to be. I made you this way. I love you so much.' I had an encounter with God. And that is why I know it is authentic." It's not an easy journey for Richard but he said that it's a series of continual steps of faith and fighting for what is right and good in God's eyes.

Richard's identity is no longer in confusion, it is now found in Christ. He has many creative skills and talents that he had used to bring glory to himself. But God has made a way for him to use them all in a way that brings God's truth to others. His passion is for the next generation. He helps lead worship and also works with children's ministry.

"I feel truly blessed that I can now speak hope into lives, sharing the truth, God's Truth. I gave my life to the Lord and never looked back. It's the most exciting, challenging journey I've been on and my life never gets dull. There is freedom, redemption, love, peace and forgiveness in Jesus Christ. That's the first act. Just remember, in any show, God orchestrates it all."

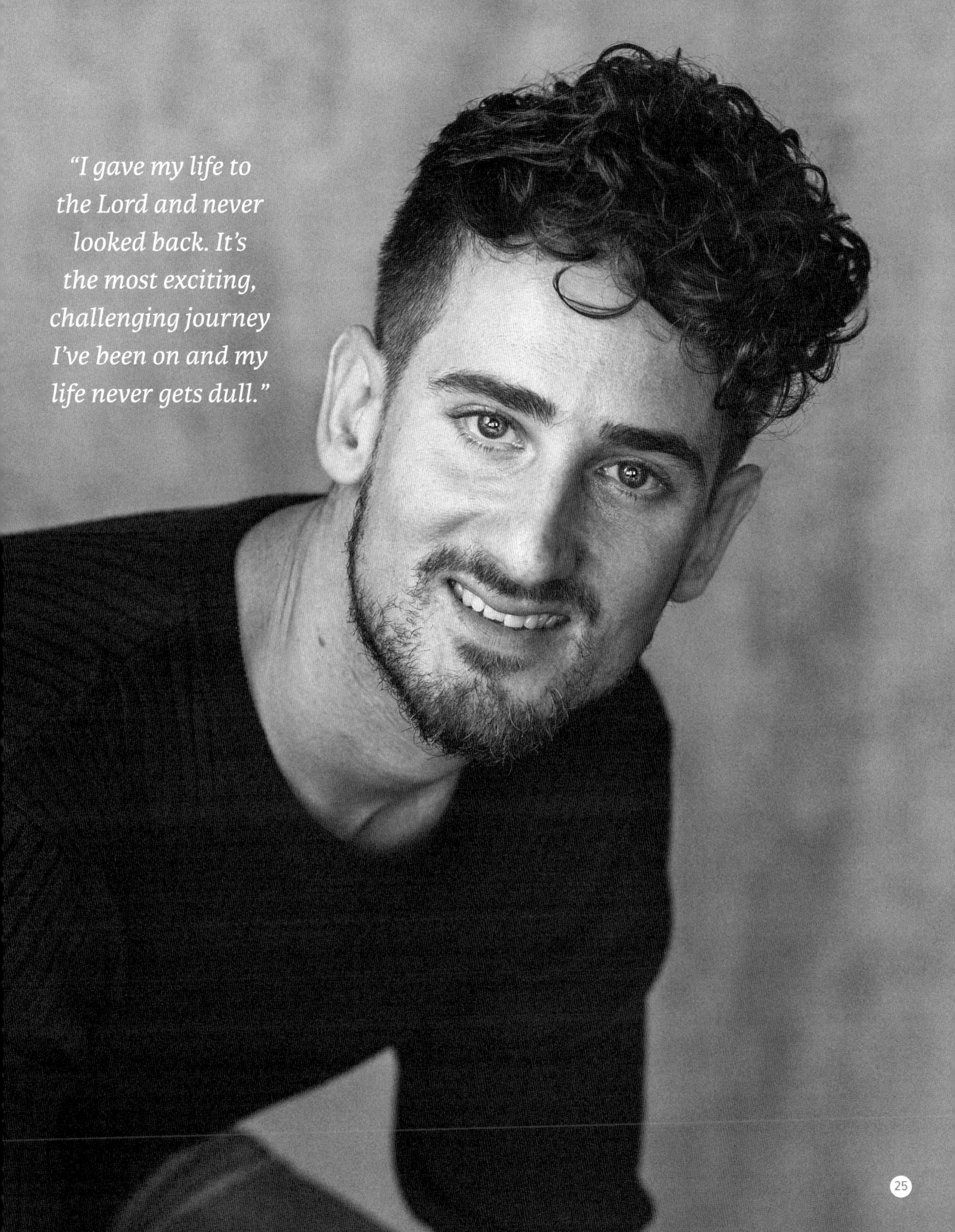
"I gave my life to the Lord and never looked back. It's the most exciting, challenging journey I've been on and my life never gets dull."

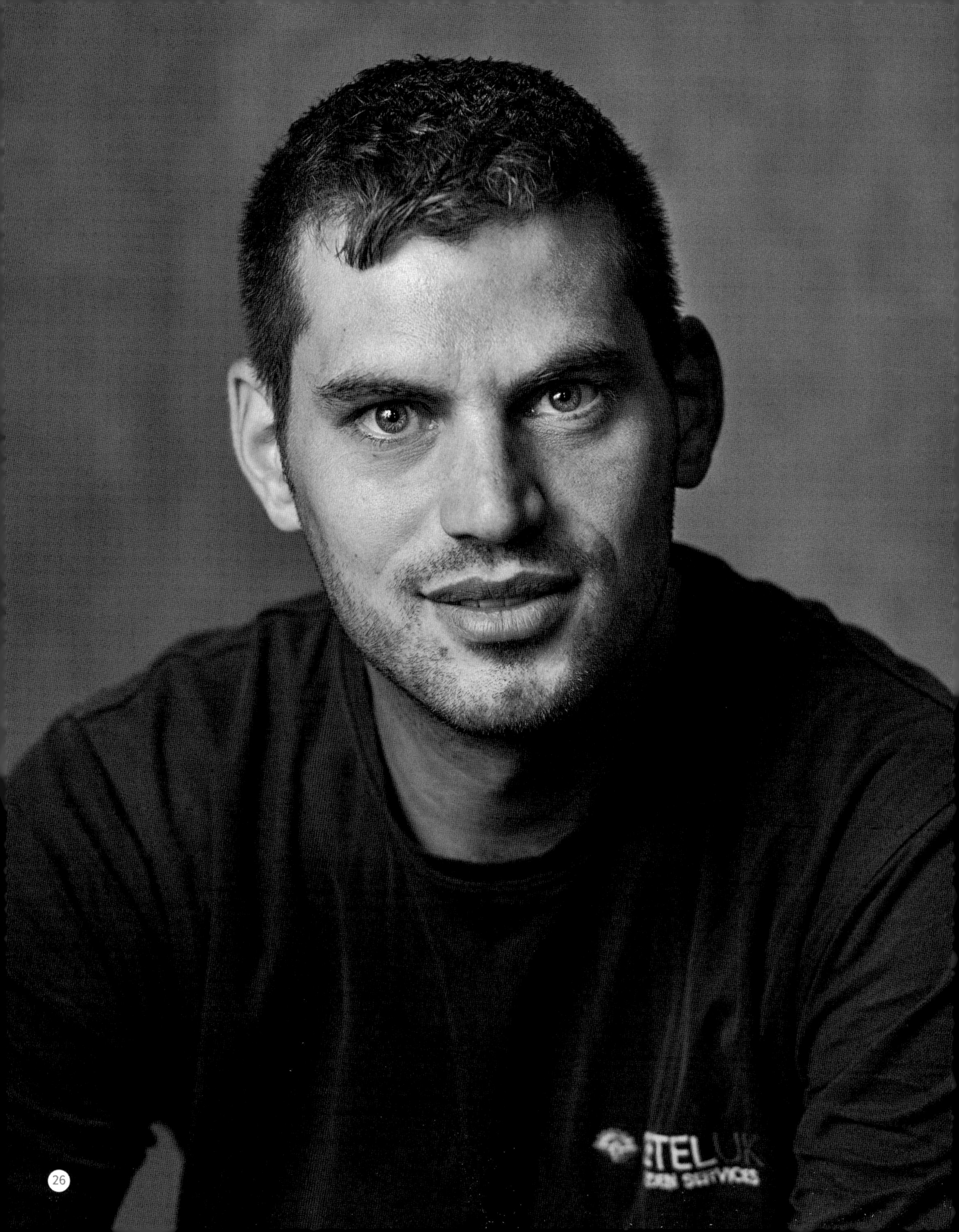

JOHN

Stokenchurch

"I had rebelled my entire life, rebelled against the world and all that it stood for. The rave[1] was the ultimate art of rebellion. We stood against the police and society. The world rejected us so we rejected it. We had created our own society. One where we made the rules and the rule was to have fun and 'stuff' the world."

Being a team leader at his job at the railway gained John an excellent wage which was all spent on his and his girlfriend's cocaine habits. "We lived in mental torture and I became a very dark version of myself. I gave up everyone for cocaine and my girlfriend." He was speeding very fast but John's world crashed to a sudden stop when he discovered his girlfriend had been stealing from him. After this he realized his life was a total fake. "I had everything you could want in life to have fun, but I felt empty and alone." Even though John used to mock his sister who was a Christian, he was suddenly curious enough to ask her about Jesus.

Attending an Alpha[2] course, he chose to give his life to Jesus. When the people at Alpha were praying for him, he suddenly felt a knot form in his stomach. It was like a well of emotion. "My emotions rose through my chest and came out of my eyes in floods of tears. I hadn't cried that much for years. I knew then that this was real, that Jesus was real."

"Since I asked Jesus into my life, things began to turn around. It looked like things were getting worse at first but He was simply trying to free me from the world and the things in it that were holding me back. I finally know who I am."

John learned that God doesn't waste anything. "The whole rebel attitude and non-conformist stuff is still in me, but I'm using it in a greater way—a totally different way because Jesus was the greatest non-conformist that ever lived! He lived and died for the truth. The truth is what I was missing my entire life. When I met Jesus that was it, I was like, 'I've found it!' I now know what I can fight for. I have something to live for, and die for."

[1]Raves were organized parties with DJs suppyling the trance- and dance-inducing music. The rave is a wave of psychedelic and other electronic dance music, most notably acid house music from Chicago, USA combined with the drug ecstasy, which developed into a new subculture called the rave. The illegal things happening at these parties quickly made the gatherings themselves illegal. Ravers were apolitical and just wanted to be free. —Wikipedia

[2]Alpha is a series of sessions exploring the Christian faith, typically run over eleven weeks. Each talk looks at a different question around faith and is designed to create conversation. Alpha programs are run all around the globe, where everyone and anyone is welcome. www.alpha.org

"I had rebelled my entire life,
rebelled against the world and all that it stood for ... "

KIRSTY

South Wales

Although Kirsty had a loving family growing up, the abuse by a family friend left her confused and changed. She kept it a secret and became a different child. The confusion of the experience changed her at a deep level. When Kirsty was 12, her older brother, who was her hero, suddenly died at 17 years of age and her life took a dangerous turn. She began smoking cannabis, which escalated to amphetamines and pills, and then on to crack and heroin. Too busy with a heroin addiction to finish school, Kirsty began to commit crimes to fund her habit.

"In the drug life you get involved with the wrong crowd; we were all drug users up to no good. Partners I had were drug users, and I was just one big mess. My life became controlled by men, drugs and crime." At 18, she barely stopped taking drugs as she gave birth to her son, only to dive deeper into her destructive lifestyle after his birth. "I couldn't even love my son because I didn't love myself. I put my family through hell but I couldn't stop taking drugs. I tried but they had a hold on me." She was in and out of her son's life as he was raised by her parents, police looking for her, stealing from family: this was the life she lived.

Things just got worse. Her mother passed away from cancer which drove her deeper still into the addictions. With her veins gone from injecting, she ended up with deep vein thrombosis (blood clots in the veins). Not even this could stop her from using. Injecting Mephedrone or M-CAT on the streets caused her to totally lose herself. The drugs she used to wash away her problems had become her prison.

Jesus met her in this lost state. Her life was totally changed once again but in an entirely new and hope-filled way. When she was so utterly desperate, Jesus came and gave her rest, peace and restoration. It only took a moment in a church meeting for her life to be altered forever. She felt something of God that was unexplainable. "Jesus showed me how to love myself and others. God has not only given me a life I never thought I would have, my dreams have come to life today all because of Jesus. I am nothing without Jesus."

Today with her son, her husband Victor and their daughter, you will find Kirsty living a restored life full of service and love for Jesus.

"Jesus showed me how to love myself and others. God has not only given me a life I never thought I would have, my dreams have come to life today all because of Jesus."

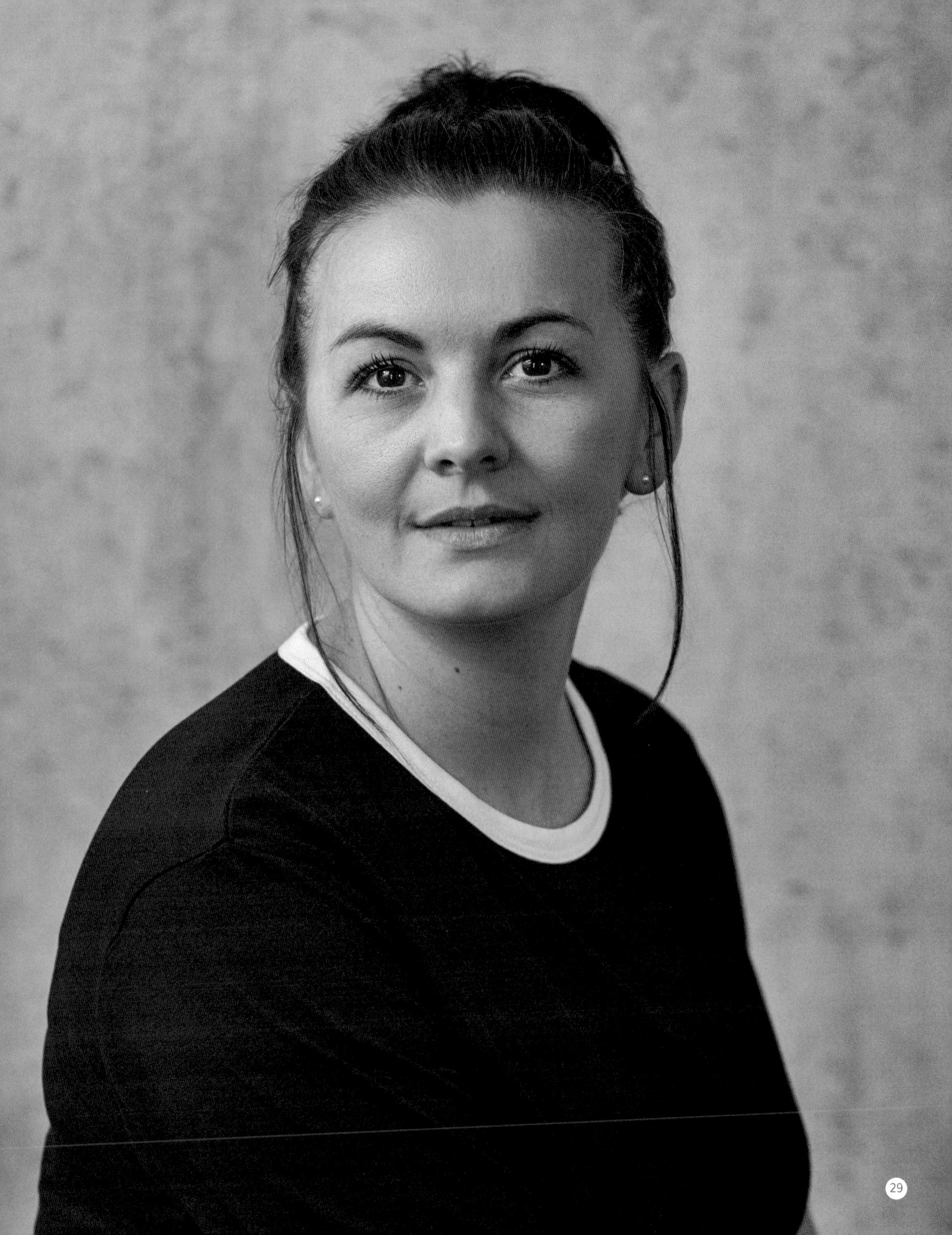

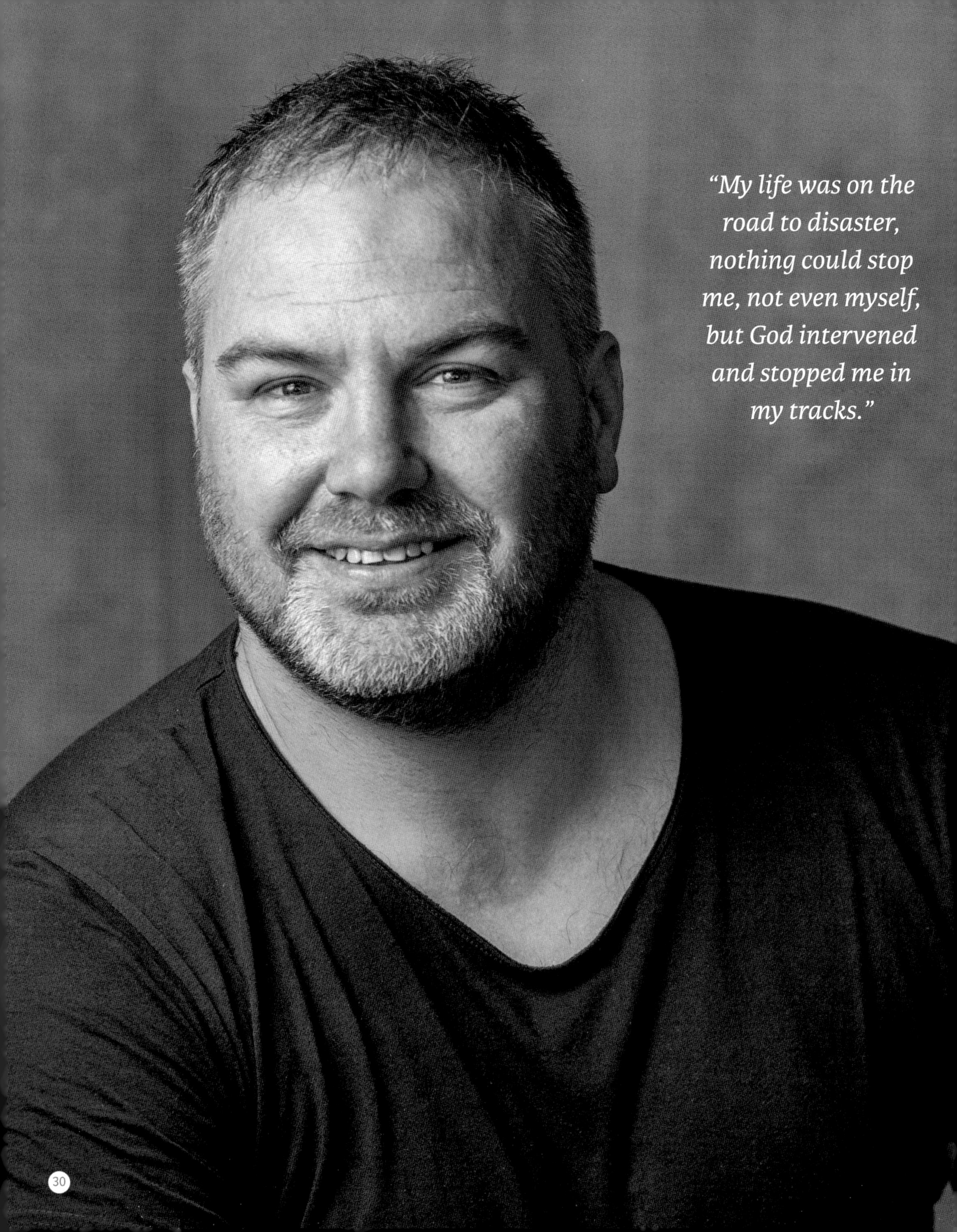

"My life was on the road to disaster, nothing could stop me, not even myself, but God intervened and stopped me in my tracks."

IAN

Nottingham

"I was fully aware of all the dangers of heroin but just didn't care anymore about life. The first time I took it, it felt like the wonder cure. All my worries and troubles went away, I felt like I could lead a normal life again. The chaos in my thinking stopped. I felt calm. My experience didn't fit the image I'd seen on TV of falling over in a pool of vomit. I felt in control and empowered. THIS is the really big lie that catches us when we use this drug. Like many others my age, we would use it to come down off other drugs; but that 'one day a week' soon became two days a week, then every other day, and eventually every day. All the way along you think you've got it under control."

Ian started drinking at 12, taking drugs daily at 14 and injecting amphetamines regularly at 17 years of age. He eventually progressed to heroin and crack. Growing up in the estates (government housing), there was a lack of male role models. Kids naturally looked to the older generation for direction and affirmation. The British rave scene of all-night parties and drugs was the culture of that older generation. The people he looked up to were very much involved in drugs.

Towards the end of his addiction, Ian had a cyst from birth that ended up getting so infected that he could barely move. Doctors determined that he needed surgery to save his life. But going from one hospital to another, he was unable to have the surgery due to the specialists not being able to get into his veins. All the heroin and crack use had damaged his veins to the point where they were completely inaccessible.

It was at this moment that Ian, who had no framework for Jesus at all, silently uttered, "I have made a mess of my life. I cannot do this. God if you're real please help me." Since he didn't even know what a prayer was, this cry was his way of calling out for something more than he knew. The next day he was transferred to another hospital and in the bed next to him was a Church of England vicar. The vicar began telling him of Jesus. A week later, after more failed attempts by specialists to ready him for the surgery he needed, his infection was gone without any treatment.

In hindsight Ian said, "I now know God healed me, and met me in that time. But I just put it down to coincidence and good antibiotics." So he carried on with drugs. The hopelessness set in again. But at 22, his dad found him and took him to Betel. Ian left after just three weeks though. "The problem was that even though I gave my life to Jesus, I was still the same negative, critical, deceitful person I was before." He left Betel for four days but remembered the freedom and life he had tasted. He wanted that more than anything.

"After stopping my drug use I had the mentality of a 14-year-old. I had avoided all the normal challenges of life that make us into adults. In my first year at Betel, God caused me to grow in responsibilities and trust, running a furniture shop." Ian is now married with a young son. God continues to knit him and Jess together as husband and wife.

"My life was on the road to disaster, nothing could stop me, not even myself, but God intervened and stopped me in my tracks. Through the love of God shining in the ministry of Betel, my life was set on track towards a wonderful future."

JESS

Malawi, Africa

For most of Jess' early life, she felt beaten down by constant bullying. The only safe place was home until her father left following an affair. Then her safety was replaced with responsibility for younger siblings and a mother who had trouble coping with the rejection and betrayal. Feeling rejected herself, Jess left home at the first opportunity.

Unfortunately, the guy she ran to introduced her to cocaine. Cocaine became like therapy to her. She had been unable to talk and process all her hurt. Cocaine enabled her to talk and get it all out, or so she thought. The deceitful bliss of drugs swiftly took her to dark and dangerous places that she couldn't handle.

Her family found Betel, and on her first night there, a woman named Tanya stayed with her until she fell asleep. But before she slept, Tanya turned to her and said, "There is something very special about you." Reflecting on what she heard Jess commented, "Those words, I hadn't heard those words in such a long, long time because of addiction." That one sentence uttered in a hushed tone brought hope like a sunrise. To think, Tanya thought she was special!

Jess's biggest victory came later in her stay at Betel. She met and married Ian and they had a lovely little boy. Together they ran a center in Watford and she was happy to be a wife and mother. But the busyness got too much for her to handle and she began secretly drinking alcohol. Instead of those around her turning away in disgust, they gathered around and fought for her and her family, giving them the support they needed to heal. Jess recalled, "Nobody had ever fought for me in my life except these people." She had wanted to run away and hide from the stuff coming up inside of her, but they showed her a better way.

Now restored to her husband and son, she is excited for the future and has begun to dream again about what God has for them. She shared, "Now, I have a greater understanding of His grace. It is no longer a concept—but a reality for my life."

"Nobody had ever fought for me in my life except these people."

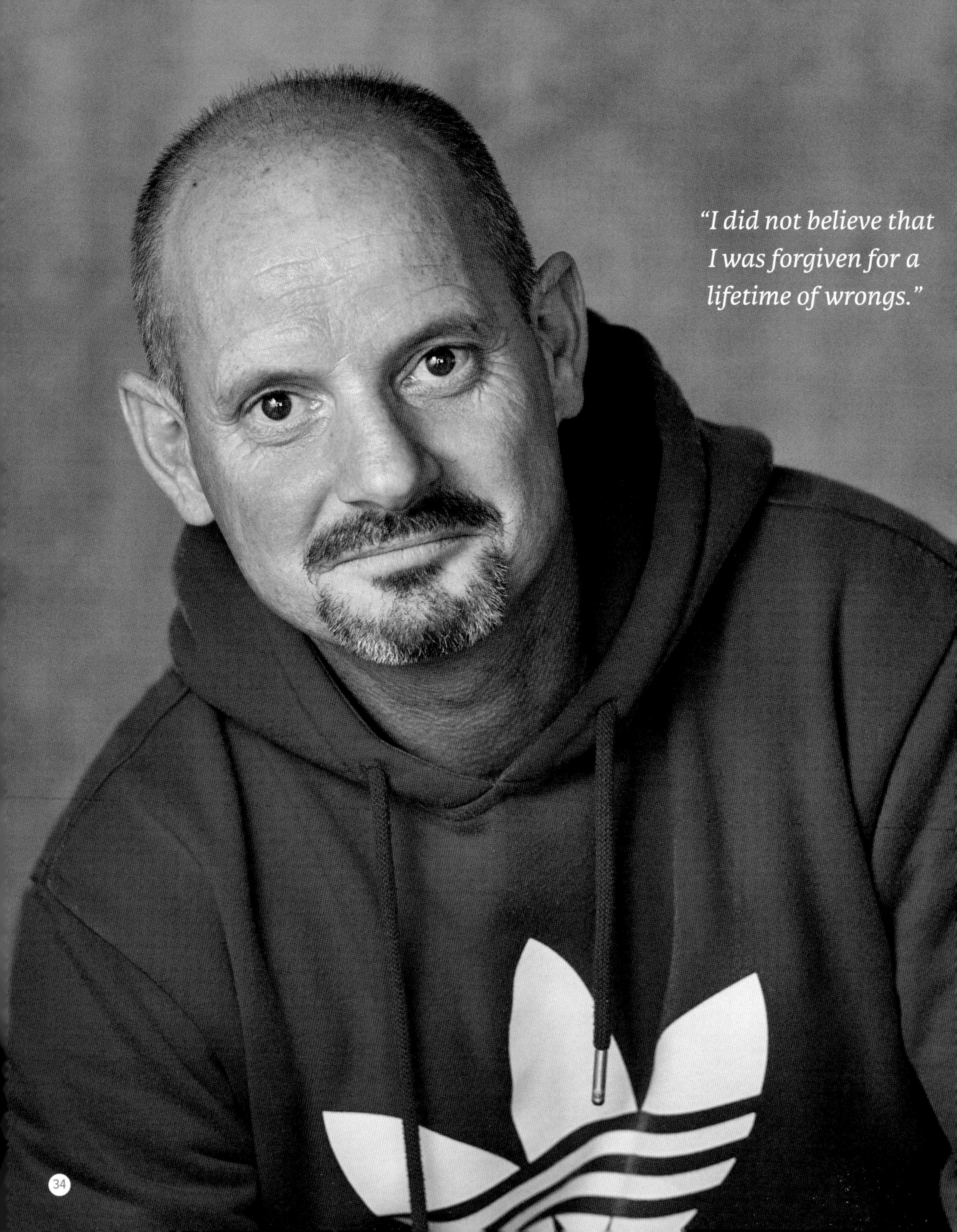
“I did not believe that
I was forgiven for a
lifetime of wrongs.”

CRAIG

Port Talbot, South Wales

Craig discovered that his dad wasn't his biological father when he was 14. This truth began his struggle with identity. After 19 years of living a lifestyle that included addiction to heroin and crack, probation, shoplifting, dealing, burglary, and car theft, Craig took on certain beliefs about himself: "I'll always be an addict" and "I'll never change, and that's the way it always will be for me."

The first time he heard about Jesus and the forgiveness Christ came to bring, Craig was offended and angry. It challenged his view of himself and of his reality. The truth that was shared that night seemed so related to him that he thought his leaders had betrayed his trust and told the speaker his personal information. But a seed of truth was planted even if he refused to let it grow much. After a short stay at Betel he chose to leave and he quickly slipped back into old habits and addictions.

"God can enter into a life in a split second," says Craig. He was withdrawing from heroin with his phone in hand. He hadn't eaten in days and had not slept in two weeks. He was waiting for his dealer to call so he could get "smack" (more heroin) from him. His phone rang but the number on the screen was unknown. Normally he wouldn't answer, but on this day he did. The man on the other end of the line was an old friend who was a part of the Betel community. "He called me 'wee man' because I'm small, and instantly I knew who it was. I broke down crying. I knew this was Jesus opening his arms to me once again." Craig decided to give the community another try.

After he returned to Betel, during the Christmas season, Craig was washing dishes and pondering the terrible things he did against his mom while addicted. She had passed away and Craig wished for her forgiveness. He was thinking and praying with Christmas music on the radio and the thought came into his head, "I wonder if my mom would be proud of me now?" In that instant the radio announcer introduced the next song, "In the Bleak Midwinter." Craig could hardly believe his ears! When he was eight years old he sang his first solo in choir and it was this song. His mom had run up to him afterward and said, 'Son, I'm so proud of you!'" He burst into tears remembering all this and felt like he was hearing his mom affirm him now.

That same Christmas his dad pulled him aside and handed him the adoption certificate and told him he didn't need a piece of paper to make him feel like a father to Craig. He had always considered him to be his true son.

Jesus has a way of answering our deepest unspoken needs.

ALLISON

London

At 24 years old, Allison had the most amazing life! She was a journalist living in a beautiful flat in West London and had a long-term boyfriend. Her life was full of parties that her friends all envied. But there were a few secrets that no one knew about. Her undisclosed life was destroying her.

In university Allison decided to part from her God-fearing upbringing and have the fun that she thought God had prevented her from experiencing. Very quickly though, she found out the truth. Her boyfriend turned from charming to controlling and abusive. All the abuse and alcohol consumption changed her self image. She no longer saw any value in herself.

Two years into the relationship with her boyfriend she got pregnant. Feeling as if there were no options for her, she aborted the baby. Full of shame and fear, she kept not only the secret of the abusive boyfriend but now the secret of the abortion. Friends and family were kept in the dark which only added to her feeling of being totally alone.

The day she had the abortion something changed. She had dreamed all her life of becoming a mother and now her life was not at all as she imagined it would be. Little by little the compromises she made took her places she never expected. In order to cope with the pain she began to drink more and more.

"By the age of 24, my life had crumbled. I was a raging alcoholic. My life was a mess and I wanted to die. I knew that if I didn't get help, I would kill myself; I couldn't see any way out of the situation I was in except suicide. I had no hope." Allison lost her job and ended up in the hospital after having an alcohol-induced fit. She told me, "I cannot describe the utter lostness and loneliness that had become my life. I had no hope."

So often when people hit rock bottom they look up. They begin to find hope again. Allison received a second chance when she found a place where she felt immediately welcomed and part of something. The women she met at Betel overwhelmed her with a sense of love. To be in a group of women and feel uplifted, encouraged and valued is rare and precious indeed.

Through the love of these women, Allison came back to God and realized something about her past relationship with Him. She had never truly known or understood the love that God had for her. He loved and accepted her and wasn't looking for her to prove anything or perform in a certain way to please Him. She was able to stop chasing fulfillment and was filled with love and acceptance by God. She said the pain of those years away from God still stings but "The journey is a process. I still mourn the loss of my baby. There is so much regret but I have been given a new life. I look forward to hopefully becoming a mother. I have a fresh start." The hope and new life she has now is evident in the immense amount of laughter that surrounds her!

Allison and Alex were married in September 2019 and are serving as a couple in Nottingham to give other broken lives real hope.

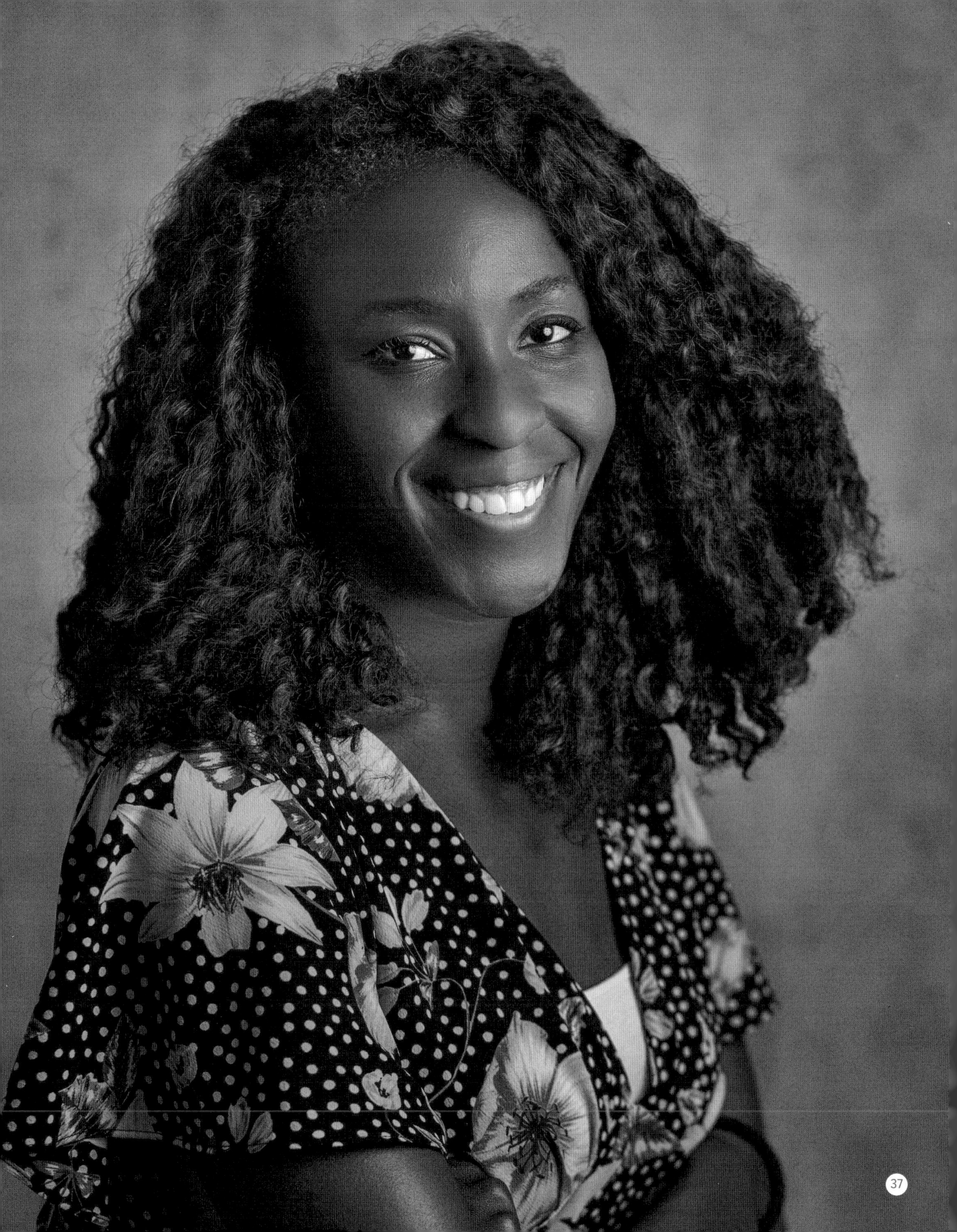

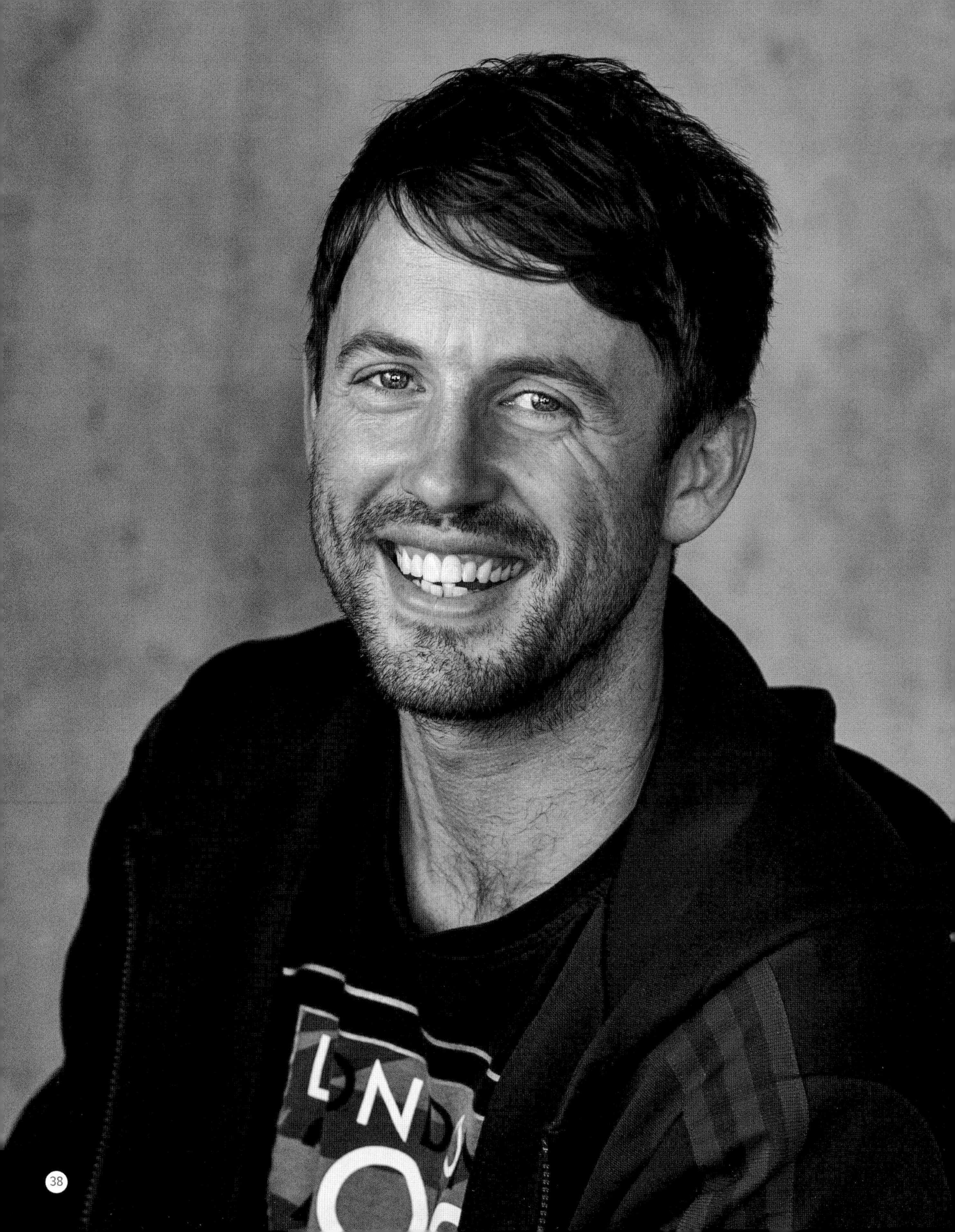

ALEX

Norwich City

“I was so fearful and so full of insecurity–feeling like I wasn’t good enough.”

Going with the crowd, Alex smoked cannabis daily starting at age 13. Heavy drinking, cocaine and other party drugs were a part of his daily life until he was 28 years old. He appeared to fit in well socially despite his addictions and he continued to function as he worked in the catering world. His career took him to Spain and various places in the UK.

At 28, he quit working and focused on his drug habit which was fueled by loneliness and depression. At one point, he woke up in a hospital after overdosing on heroin which only piled more depression on his deep hopelessness. He thought, “Now for another go around on the Tragic Roundabout of my life!” But in that moment, wanting to give up on everything, God brought about something unexpected.

One by one, members of a family from his past began to come visit him in the hospital. He hadn’t seen them for 18 years or more. They began to talk to him about Jesus and how to get the help he needed. So Alex decided to give Jesus and Betel a try.

Sometimes when we are surrounded by Christians it is easy to talk the talk and appear to have it all together. This was how Alex spent the next year of his life basically putting on an act. It was when Alex’s fun stories and anecdotes ran out that he heard Jesus speak to his heart. What he heard brought deep healing to him, “You’re enough. I chose you, I called you, I love you.” Those words made it possible for him to sit in silence, to not have to have the last word and find another witty thing to say. He could just be himself. He realized he actually wasn’t designed to fit into the world, he was designed for relationship. Alex told me, “It wasn’t an altar call that saved me, it was a deep spiritual thirst.” This thirst is what keeps him going towards God and others, enabling him to connect and grow.

“You’re enough. I chose you, I called you, I love you.”

MICHAEL

Manchester

Michael's life followed this pattern: believer in God, agnostic, atheist, believer, alcoholic, and finally follower of Jesus. His journey included many different belief systems as he went through life. When he started drinking in his 30s, he didn't intend to take the path he took. It slowly moved into deep alcoholism. His parents ended up banning him from their home for three years because of his behavior.

Michael lost his job, got into debt, and drank cheap alcohol. He told me that he considered his choices to be worse than so many other guys' because he had known God before and walked away from Him. This kind of thinking only made him feel even more distant from forgiveness, God and his family.

The amazing thing about Jesus is that He never walks away no matter what choices we make. The day Michael decided to get help and go to Betel, something crazy happened. To get up the courage to enter Betel, he took a bunch of sleeping tablets and Librium (a drug used to produce a calming effect) and washed it all down with lots of alcohol. In the past, if he tried to stop drinking cold turkey, he would have been afraid to leave his bed for fear of the extreme physical withdrawal symptoms. But this time, with his decision to follow Jesus and give the community of Betel a try, he woke the next morning feeling a bit rough, but no hangover, no shaking, no normal withdrawal symptoms.

Years have passed since that day and many other freedoms have come Michael's way. Michael now shares the gospel through teaching and preaching. He encourages people in a quiet but profound way.

Michael's journey included many different belief systems as he went through life.

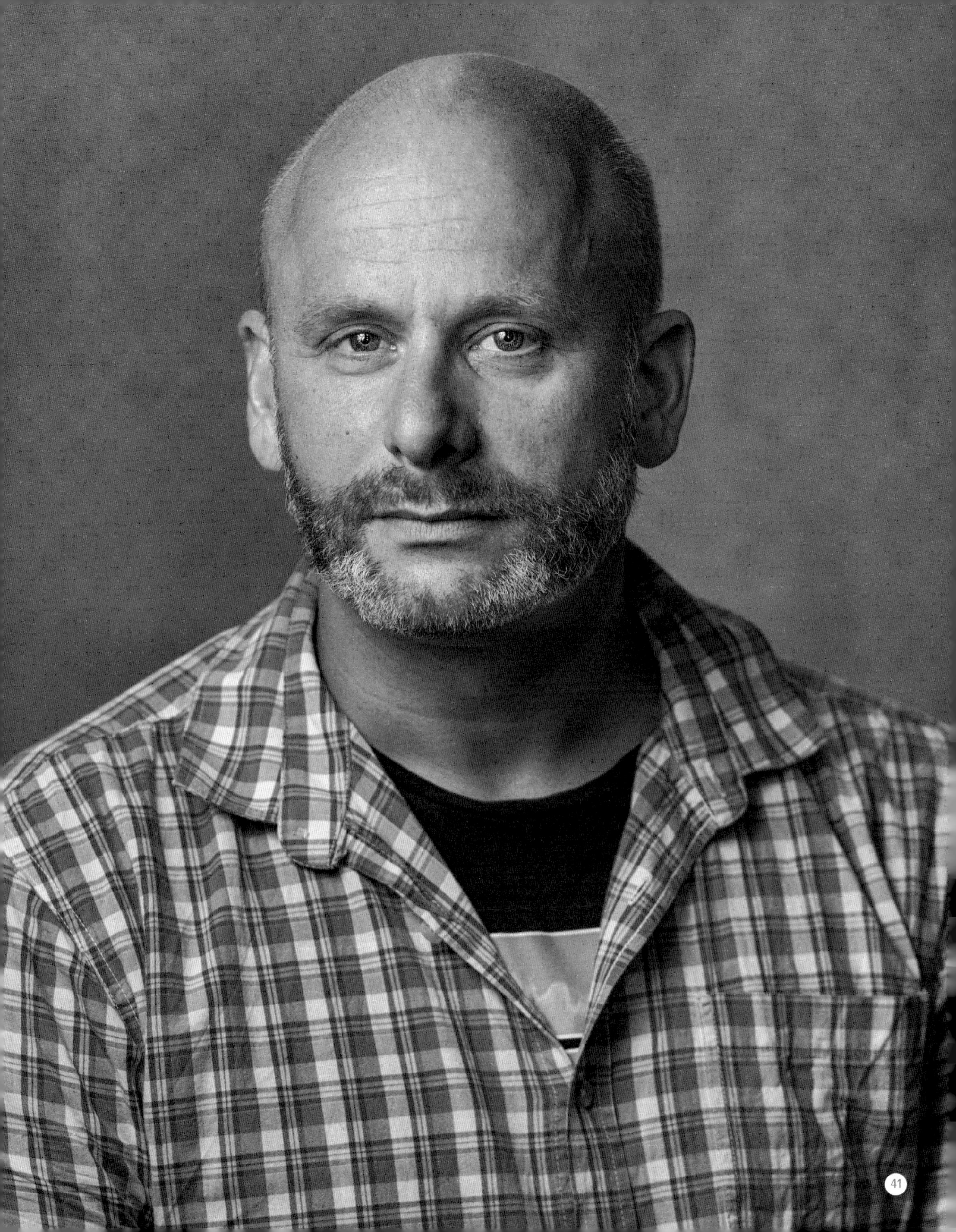

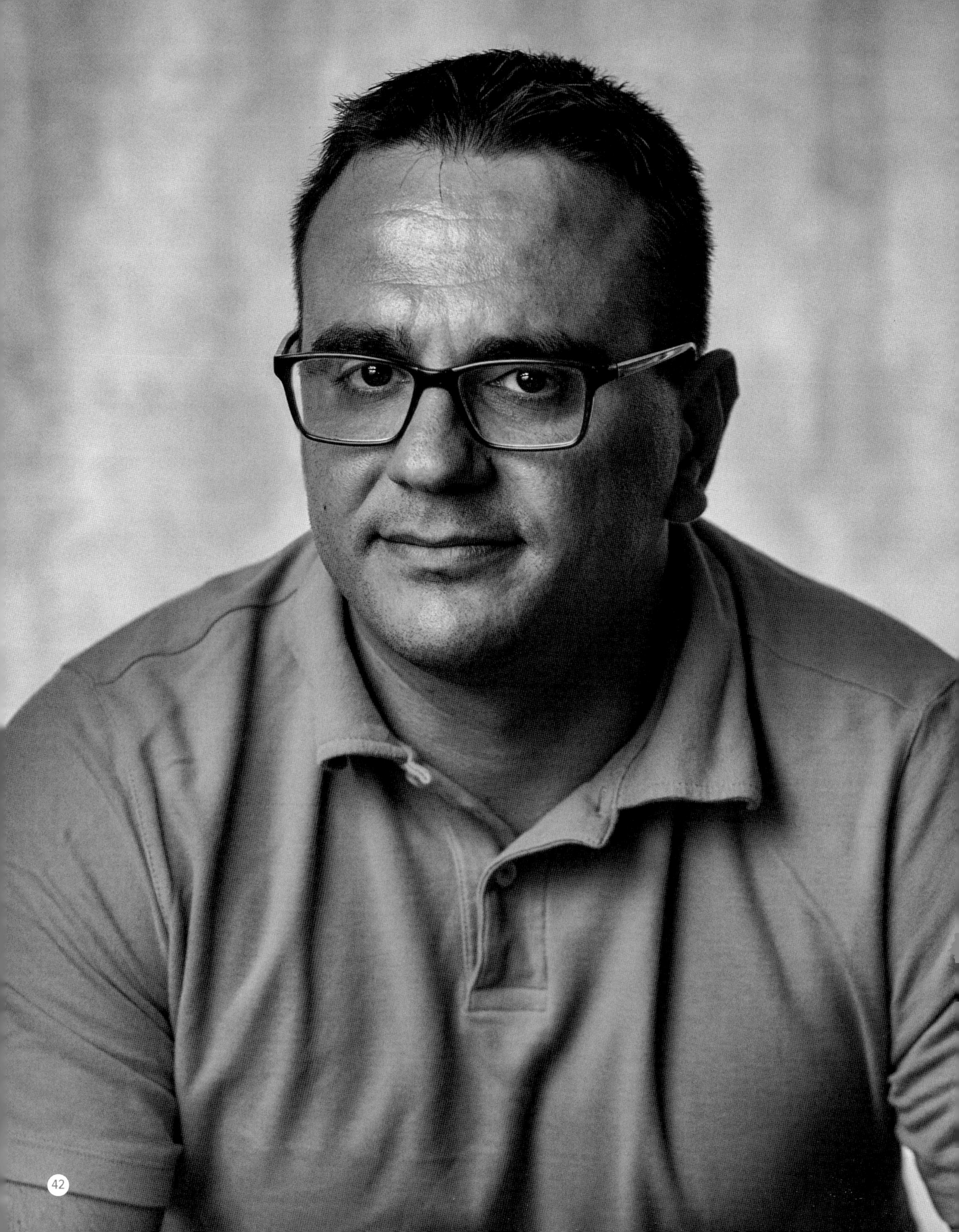

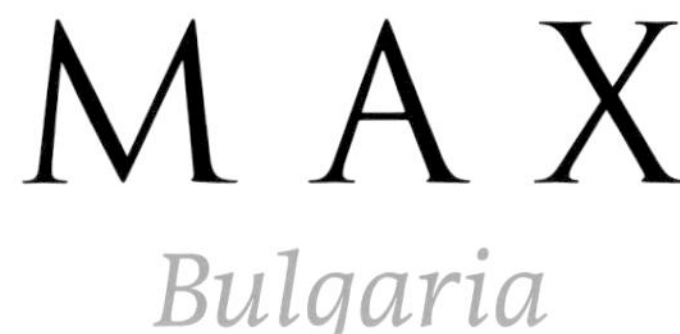

MAX

Bulgaria

Max started taking drugs when he was 12 years old. Later at university he escalated to harder drugs and finally was on heroin at 23. Upon completing his schooling, his career in information technology was coupled with taking drugs. He truly didn't see himself living past his 30s, which caused him to live recklessly.

Nearing 30 years of age, he became conscious of his need to live differently. He moved to the UK to find support. Soon after entering Betel, Max was sitting cross-legged on the floor enjoying the music, but not wanting anything to do with the Jesus the others in the room were singing about. Someone came up behind him and touched his shoulder and began to pray for him. He didn't care what they were saying or who they were. He simply wasn't interested in Jesus or what He had to offer. But all of a sudden he felt intense joy and couldn't stop smiling. He tried to force his mind to think about his old way of life that he had been craving since he left it a few months ago. He tried to think about the drugs, drink, and women who had consumed him before but something in his mind wouldn't even let him linger there at all. He said it was as if his mind totally excluded any thoughts concerning his past. "I was just full of joy and all I could think of in that moment was how good life is ... how good God is!" This is when he realized something very different was happening to him. That night a door was opened to something more, something freeing.

Ten months after moving to the UK, Max had a thought about what his life could be in 50 years and it literally stopped him in his tracks. The idea was so foreign that he stood still while the thought formulated. "I've never thought about living that long. I didn't think I'd reach 30 years the way I was going." The concept of living a long time, loved, accepted, and forgiven with a purpose had never been in his mind until that very moment. It changed everything for him.

Max and his wife Holly happily serve in Betel Darby where he leads worship and is using his IT skills to help run Betel's national furniture website.

"I was just full of joy and all I could think of in that moment was how good life is ... how good God is!"

HOLLY

Lymm

"Nothing could ever satisfy. Something was always missing."

Smoking and drinking from a very early age, Holly continued this lifestyle through all her schooling years as she prepared to become a dental nurse. Drinking and clubbing every weekend quickly turned into drinking every day. In her early 20s, in a space of just a few weeks, she lost everything: her home, her job, and her driver's license. Her friends and family wanted nothing to do with her anymore because of the excessive drinking. Given an ultimatum of prison or Betel, she chose the latter.

Holly had been searching her whole life for something to fill her. When talking to me about her past she said, "I was trying to receive love from something else that is materialistic (drugs or alcohol). This would only satisfy me for a short time until I had to do it again." The deception of alcohol is that it fills a void. But as Holly said, she had to do it again and again and again. The addiction was insatiable. When she discovered God's love it filled the place in her life that was perpetually empty. She expressed it this way, "The love from the Lord is there constantly."

Eventually Holly realized she had someone in her life she was unable to forgive. As she thought about the life she had led and yet still felt forgiven by Jesus, she had an epiphany. She felt that she could now release the person who had wronged her. She felt heavy and weighed down for years because of the pain, bitterness, and unforgiveness but as she let forgiveness flow from her, she felt God's love come over her. Holly exclaimed, "I felt lighter, pure! I felt clean, and as I looked in the mirror and saw my eyes were so blue, it was like I felt purified. The forgiveness washed the heaviness and bitterness away."

"One thing I can be certain of and secure in is—I have hope in my heart and a future in Him. He pulled me out of darkness into the light and for that I will be forever grateful."

I have hope in my heart and a future in Him. He pulled me out of darkness into the light and for that I will be forever grateful."

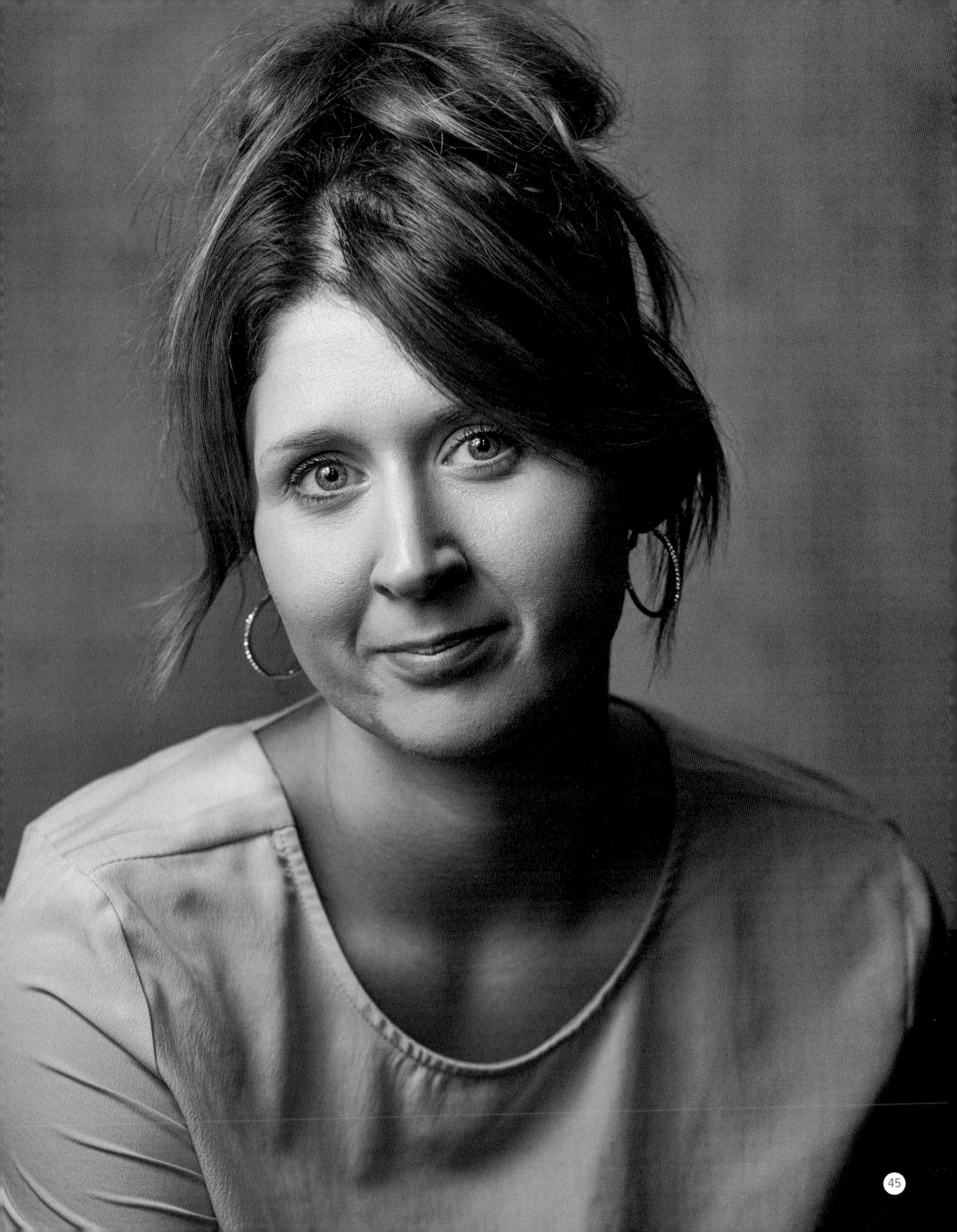

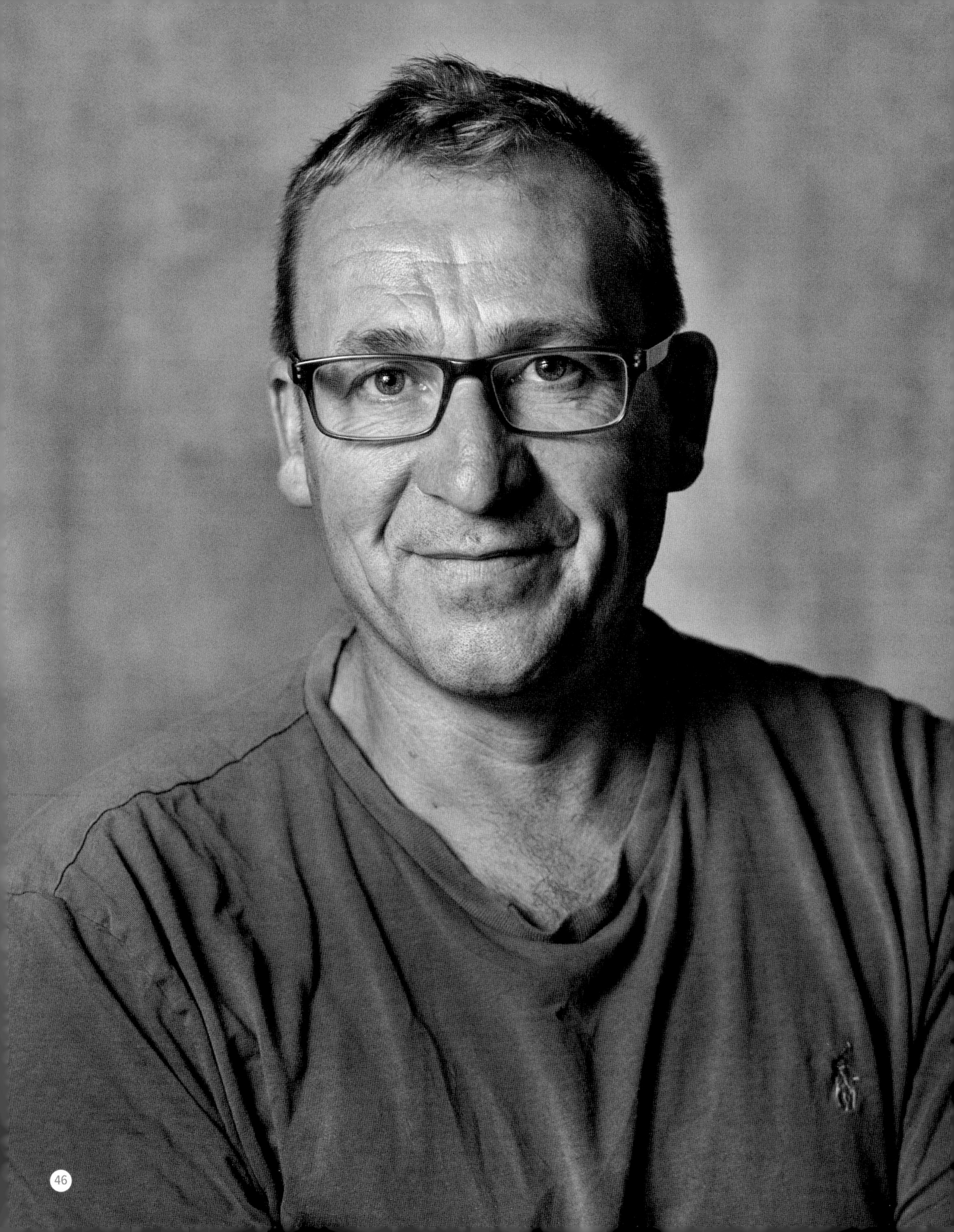

DAVE

Oxford

Drugs and alcohol were a tool for Dave. Being shy and fearful, the substances made it possible for him to relate to people around him. Due to the substance abuse, Dave experienced psychosis and it put him in a cycle of depression. The rehab would only give six months of funding for help and he knew he needed more time than that to get well. Again, he felt hopeless.

Then he found a community of people who accepted him for who he was. This place also ticked off the boxes of what he needed: it was free, unlimited stay, and no prerequisites to coming in. He didn't come in looking for God—just freedom from the pain. In the end, he decided to give Jesus a try because he felt that otherwise he would probably die by his own hand. Nothing else had worked.

Much of Dave's life has been a process of just getting from one place to another. Dave says God turned around situations in his life to "bring about a little mettle in him," most of them in the form of his journey and everyday choices. For someone who had been known as the "most depressed person" at Betel, Jesus changed his focus and gave him endless possibilities. Dave no longer feels like everything leads to the end for him. "Jesus was the beginning for me," he said. Dave is constantly renewing his mind in Christ to keep his focus on the truth.

Now married with two lovely children, Dave is a Betel pastor, teacher, leader, and encourager. "I have dreams to come yet; I'm on an adventure."

"I have dreams to come yet; I'm on an adventure."

ADRIAN

Nuneaton

"I came to Betel to give up drinking, I had no idea God was going to change me."

At one point in Adrian's life he had it all: fancy house, boat and everything he needed or wanted. But time found him three times divorced due to his alcohol abuse and the mental torment he put his ex-wives through. One morning he sat in his car in a field having stolen red wine for breakfast. Cigarettes rolled from butts picked up off the street were strewn across his dash. His socks, which hadn't been changed in three weeks, aired out on a tree just beyond his car. He was washing himself with baby wipes and he thought, "What am I doing?! I'm a Sergeant in the Air Force! I had better do something or I'm going to be dead!"

Months later after entering Betel, Adrian was asked to lead devotions for a group of guys in the community. He lay in bed and simply asked God, "Give me something to share." The answer came, surprisingly, in a nightmare. He was taken through his military past and shown how he treated the women in his life. He even saw a girl named Jackie whose hair he used to pull as a schoolboy! At 3:00 a.m. he awoke crying and shaking. He got out of bed, got on his hands and knees, and for the first time he truly repented for what he had done. At that moment, his faith jumped from his head to his heart, deep into him. He told me, "I felt it go: from that moment everything changed. How I felt, how I reacted, the peace I felt."

All his life, Adrian's actions had been controlled by his emotions and his anger. After this change, he began to be aware of his reactions and was able to choose a healthy response. "Because of this change, I know Christ is changing me."

Once when he was struggling with forgiving himself for the years of bad choices, a friend asked him, "Do you truly believe in God? If you believe God has truly forgiven you, then who on earth are you to not forgive yourself? Get on with it!" At this, Adrian said his guilt and shame left. "I know God loves me, He always has, and He forgave me then and forgives me now. I truly trust in the Lord. I have forgiven myself and am at peace with the Lord, content and happy."

Adrian's desire is to stay at Betel and help the younger men experience the freedom that comes from Christ. He said if he can help just one person, it is worth it all.

"I came to Betel to give up drinking,
I had no idea God was going to change me."

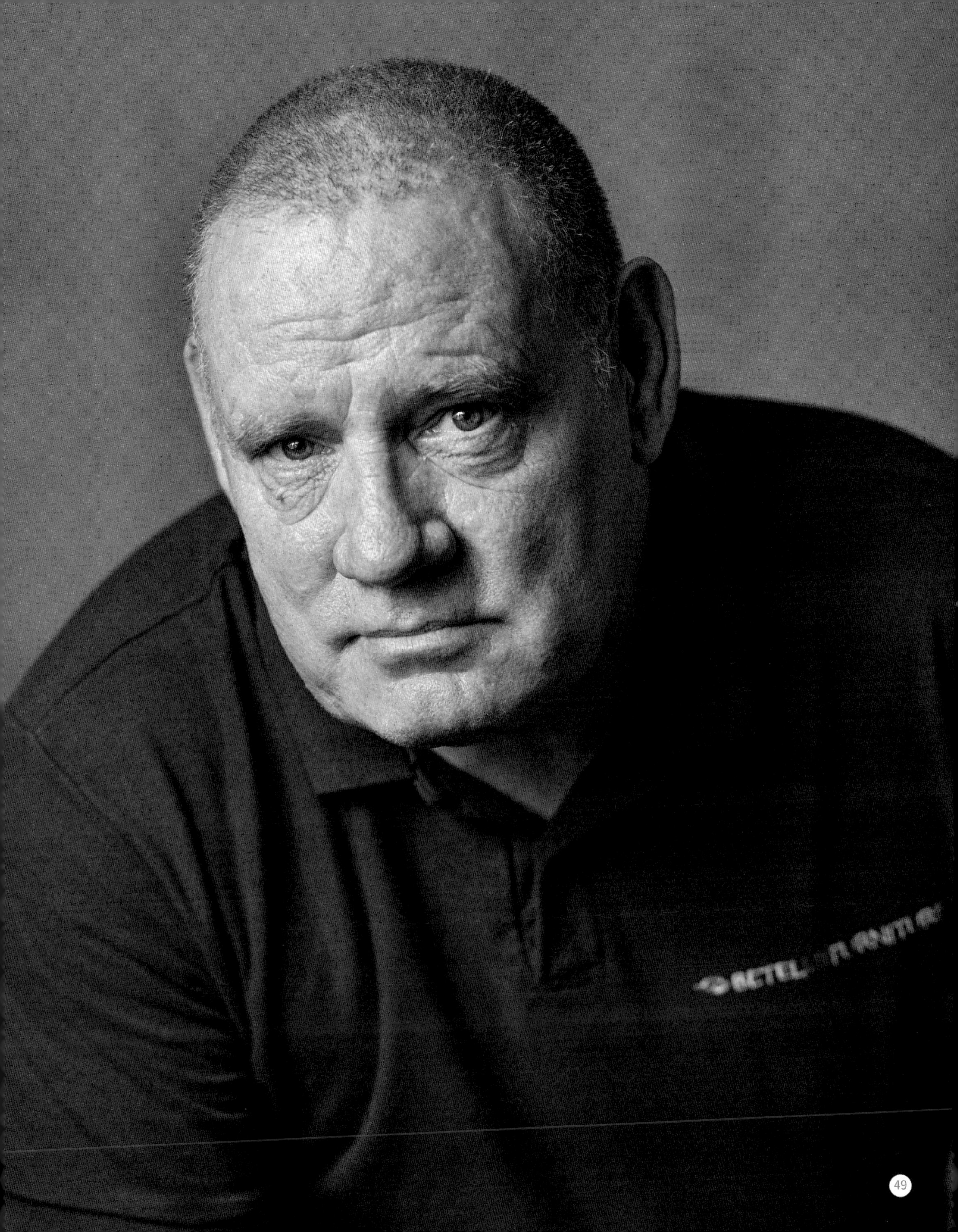

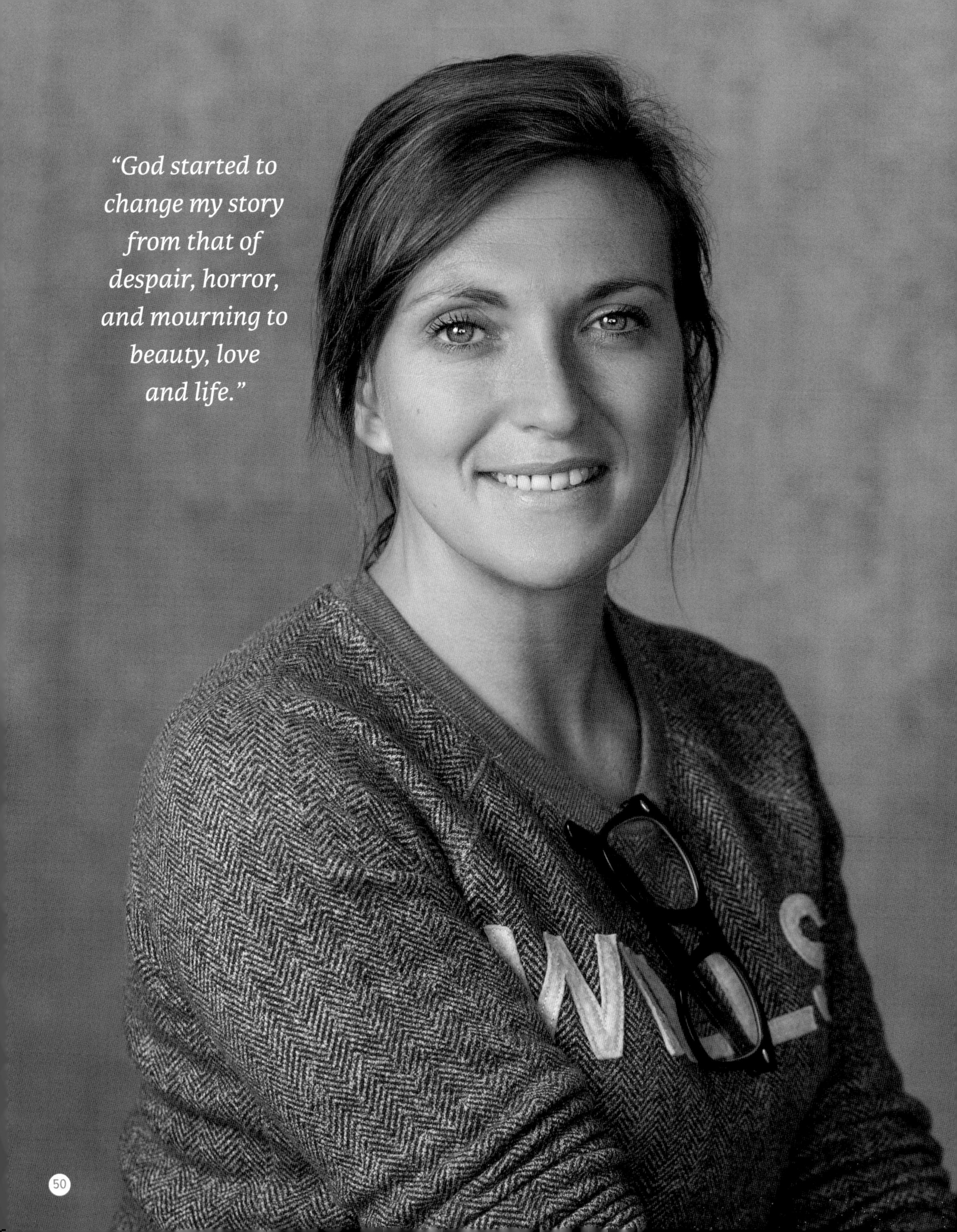

"God started to change my story from that of despair, horror, and mourning to beauty, love and life."

CERI

Wales

"God has breathed new life into my bones. I had no life. I was spiritually dead and practically physically dead too, but now I have new life and He is renewing my spirit day by day."

At age 12 Ceri started taking cannabis, amphetamines, cocaine, and ecstasy due to exposure to drugs from her uncle and his friends. She organized parties and supplied drugs to her peers through her uncle. "I found my identity in being the party girl who supplied everyone with what they needed. But I was unhappy. I felt empty and kept searching for fulfillment through an extreme lifestyle."

Due to the intense stresses in her early 20s she began smoking heroin which she always swore she'd never do. "As soon as I smoked it, I felt like all my troubles, all my stress and anxiety just melted away completely. The heroin numbed all my feelings. I fell in love with it."

Spending £100-£150 a day on heroin, she started to run out of money. All it took was one conversation for Ceri to become a full-time escort. This opened a door to an even deeper world of darkness. She said to me, "All my morals, dignity and self-respect went out the window." The other drugs weren't enough to cover her agony so she added crack cocaine to her list of pain killers which fractured her mental health to a new low. Just when she thought things in her life couldn't possibly get any worse, she was introduced to injecting amphetamines. She described, "Before I knew it, I had a full-on needle fixation and got completely consumed by that too. By this point my looks for escorting had faded and I needed to find a different way of making money. So I started to deal amphetamines and heroin."

"I was trapped in this hell and didn't even want to exist anymore. All family relationships had completely broken down. I held no regard for anyone or anything." Soon after this Ceri came to Betel and she said, "God started to change my story from that of despair, horror, and mourning to beauty, love and life."

After meeting Jesus, Ceri began an amazing journey of restoration. She told me, "I wanted everything that He had to offer. I was desperate for that deep rebuilding which needed to happen in me and my family too." In just four-and-a-half years, God has restored relationships with her family and friends. The deep inner healing Ceri needed is in full swing now. Despite being so unrecognizable by the end of all the chaos, weighing only seven stone (98lbs) and covered with stab marks, bruises, and scars all over her legs and arms, she amazingly has very few visible scars left.

"I used to be selfish, devious, manipulative, angry and very bitter. But God has come and slowly melted my heart with His love. I live for Him now. I owe Him everything and I love living to please God."

PAUL

Sunderland

"No one cared and they were glad to get rid of me."

Paul worked for a large pharmaceutical firm and had controlled his drinking for many years, but it slowly began to creep up on him. "Everything went from bad to worse and my wife and our two children hated me. Legal cases arose, I went to prison, came out and drank even more."

A Christian woman who owned the local newsstand (convenience store) noticed Paul's need for help. She and her husband pursued him until he was ready to accept their assistance. "It took several weeks to even start to look human again. I could not hold a cup up to drink tea as my shaking and lack of coordination stopped me," Paul said.

Now, years in Betel, after becoming healthy and whole, Paul tells of the time his ears were opened. He was mostly deaf but didn't regard the hearing loss as a problem and accepted someone praying for healing anyway. The next day he was in a hurry and ran off to work without his hearing aids. At noon he realized he could hear perfectly well. He says, "This time I got a physical gift from God, as opposed to a spiritual gift."

One of the most important things to Paul now is the relationship he has with his two children, one where he can encourage and help them in their lives. "I've been restored to my children and I have a good relationship with them now."

"I've been restored to my children and I have a good relationship with them now."

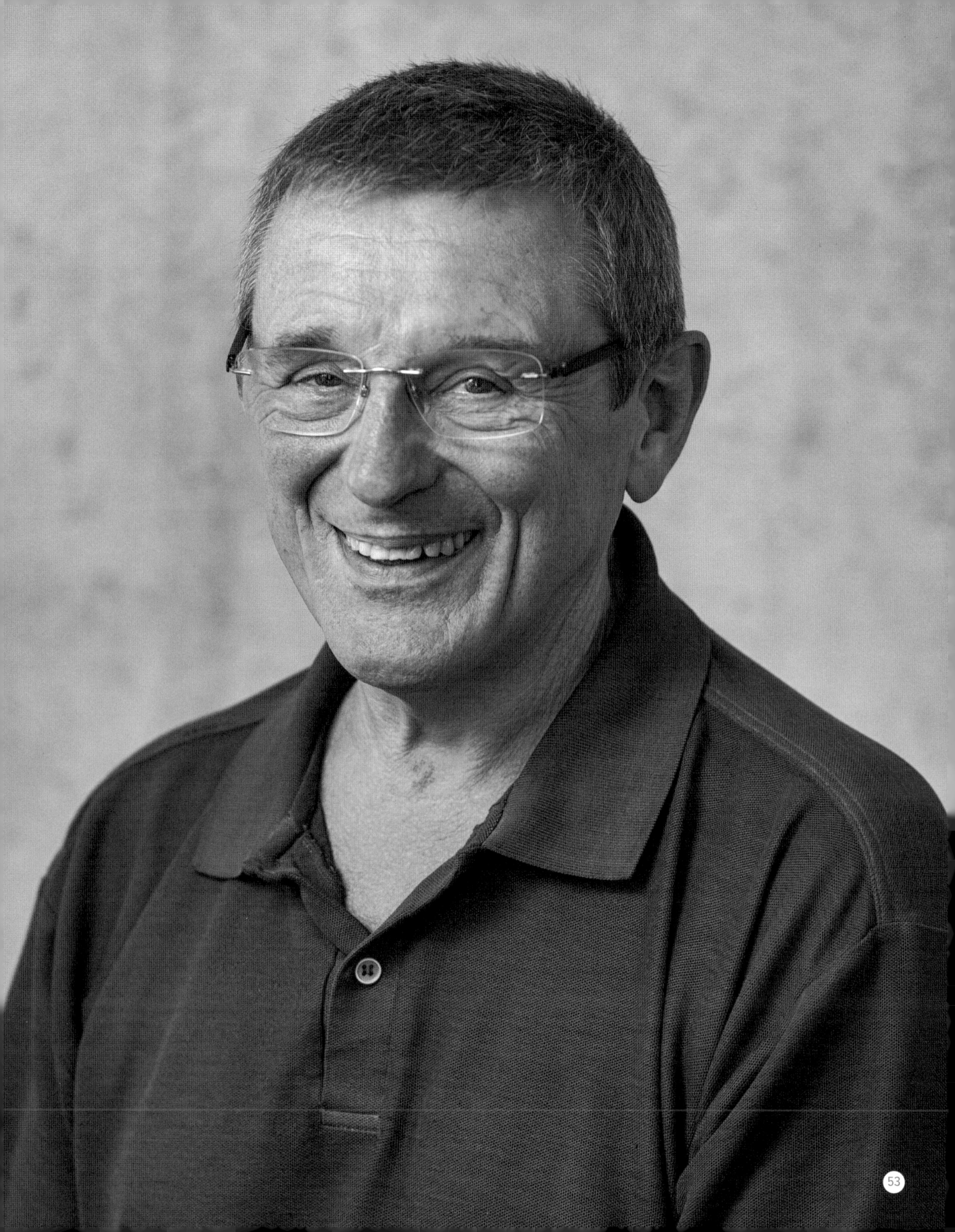

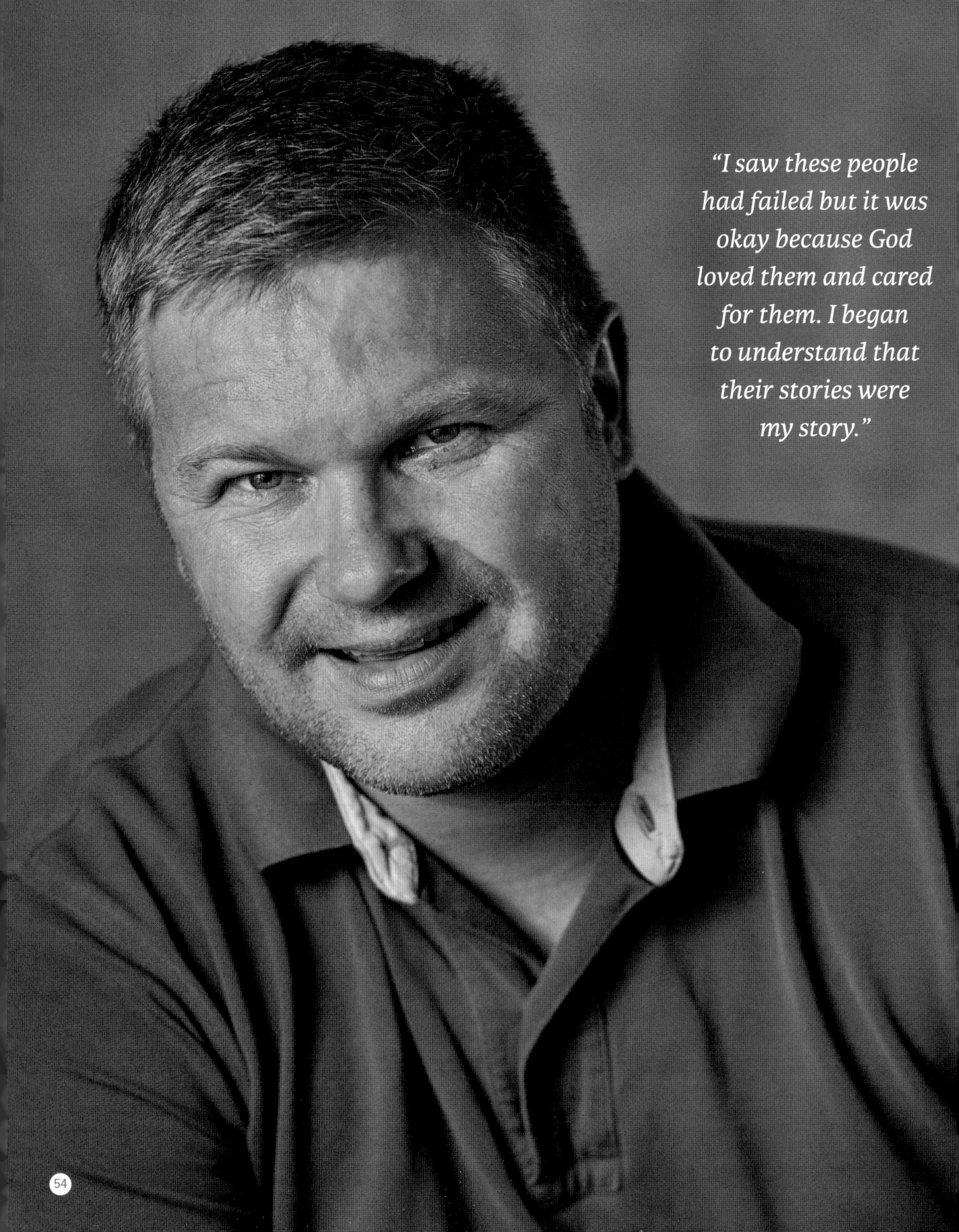
"I saw these people had failed but it was okay because God loved them and cared for them. I began to understand that their stories were my story."

ANTHONY

Nottingham

"I had no veins left in my body so I injected heroin in my neck. On one occasion I let somebody else do that. It was a missed hit and it ate my shoulder away. I could barely lift my arm up; I couldn't lift it behind me, it was completely shot. One day I was in the bath thinking, 'This (shoulder) will never be right ... unless maybe God can heal it.' "

As a kid, Anthony wanted to be like his dad, who was a good man. He wrongly perceived that his dad's acceptance of him was connected to Anthony's performance. In actuality there was no pressure put on him by his father, he realized much later. As Anthony told me, "My fear of failure became crippling and I needed an escape. I put way too much pressure on myself."

Anthony excelled at school and sports but there was never enough success for him; he craved something more. "I discovered drugs, soft drugs at first, always vowing to never go any further, but up the ladder I climbed as I sought greater and greater highs and escapes." As his drug use escalated so did his feeling of success. He felt the intoxication of success itself in using and selling drugs.

The first use of crack and heroin wasn't as exciting or as heady as he thought it would be but he was compelled to try again. This second time, his world moved. "You see I had found a place where it didn't matter what anyone thought. Little did I realize how dark and lonely a place that would become but it was true, it didn't matter because the pain and failings of life disappeared—at least for a time."

After losing a long-term girlfriend, Anthony began to inject heroin instead of smoking it and at this point his world ended. What he thought he controlled, now had full control of him. After a time, his desperation to get clean led him to get help.

At Betel, Anthony met Jesus through the love and care of people just like him. They had different circumstances but they had experienced the same lifestyle. But now they were happy, at peace, and possessed a newfound inexpressible joy and love for life. He found that Jesus changes everything. "I saw these people had failed but it was okay because God loved them and cared for them. I began to understand that their stories were my story. I understood that Jesus made it alright, that I didn't have to be perfect or succeed in everything. Jesus had died for me personally to deal with my shortcomings. He didn't excuse them but he dealt with them anyway."

Looking at Anthony today you would never notice even a slight issue with his shoulder. The healing of his deteriorated shoulder wasn't instantaneous. But slowly and surely the muscle redeveloped. He regained sensation and has full mobility.

Anthony told me that he, his wife, four children and granddaughter are privileged to see God do incredible things all the time. "We see so much of His goodness in what we do. At times we can take it for granted and we just presume on Him. We are exposed to the wonder of God's redemptive and healing power all the time."

MALCOLM

Hamilton North Lanarkshire

"In my lifetime I've had many highs, but too many lows and one rock bottom."

Malcolm has a quick smile with an obvious joy that seeps out of him. He grew up with supportive parents who gave him all the opportunities he could ever want. They set him up for achievement in academics, sports and the arts. He went on to be very successful, first in a government position and then in the private business world. He came to a point in his life where he had everything.

But through all the success, he told me he was "not satisfied with life." So he sought solace in alcohol. In his search for satisfaction, Malcom tried everything he could get his hands on. Money didn't bring satisfaction. More women only made things worse. His wife divorced him and took his child with her and out of his life. He spent some time in prison for tax evasion, and when he was released he proceeded to drink his way to the very bottom.

Totally broken, and on crutches, with only gray flannel shorts, a t-shirt and sandals to his name, Malcolm hit rock bottom. This is how he came to the door of Betel. Up to this point he had tried all types of local service providers to stop drinking—with no success. He told me, "I knew nothing about how to live a full life." Once at Betel he met people who had very similar life stories, only they seemed to have a peace that he needed. It was what he had been searching for his whole life.

When you speak with Malcolm now, you truly can see a glint in his eye that draws you in to ask, "What do you have that makes you shine?" He is keen to share that the peace and joy he has found is from chasing after Jesus.

"I can see the miracle that I am here, so nothing is impossible. I was hopeless, but in Jesus I've got hope."

"In my lifetime I've had many highs,
but too many lows and one rock bottom."

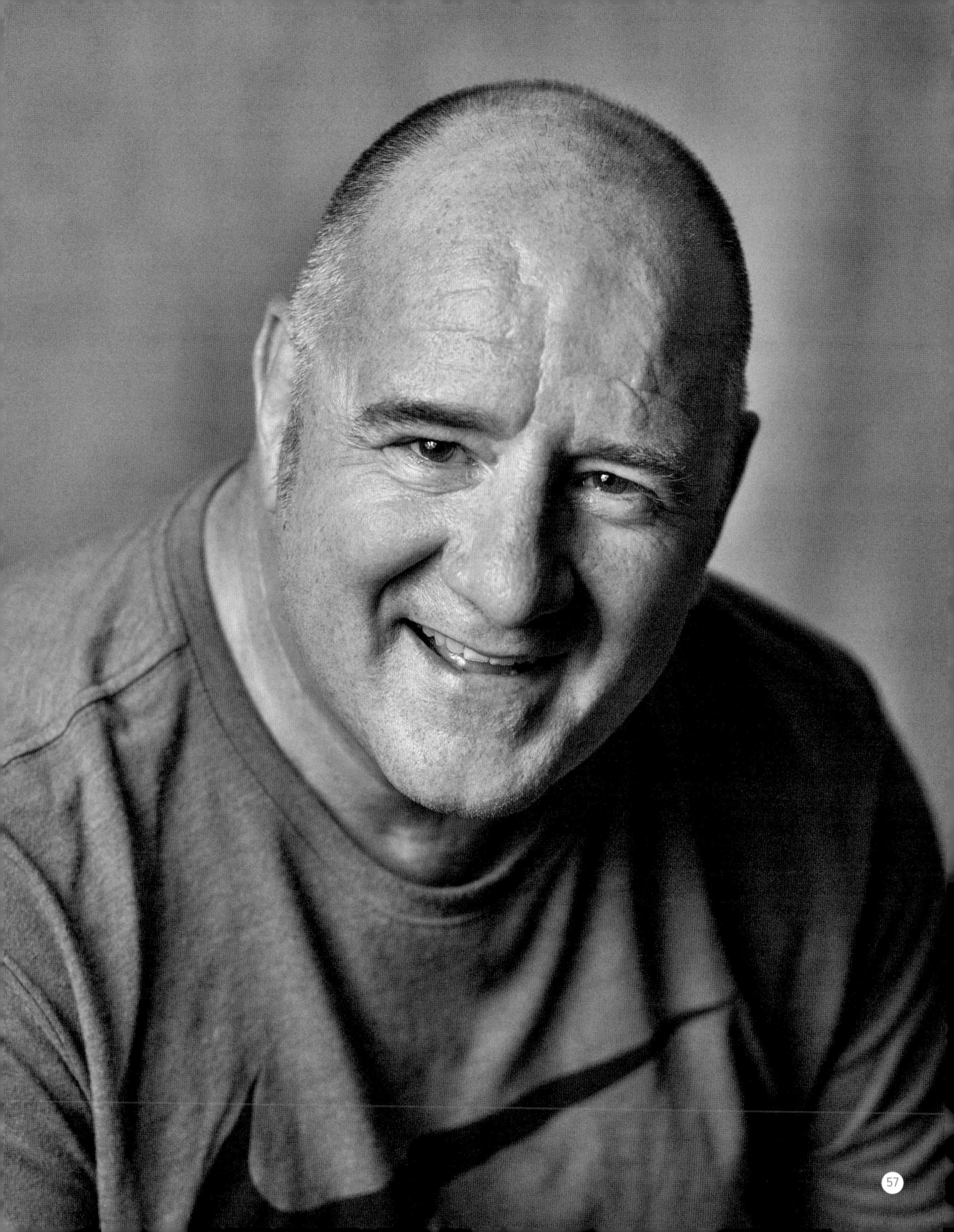

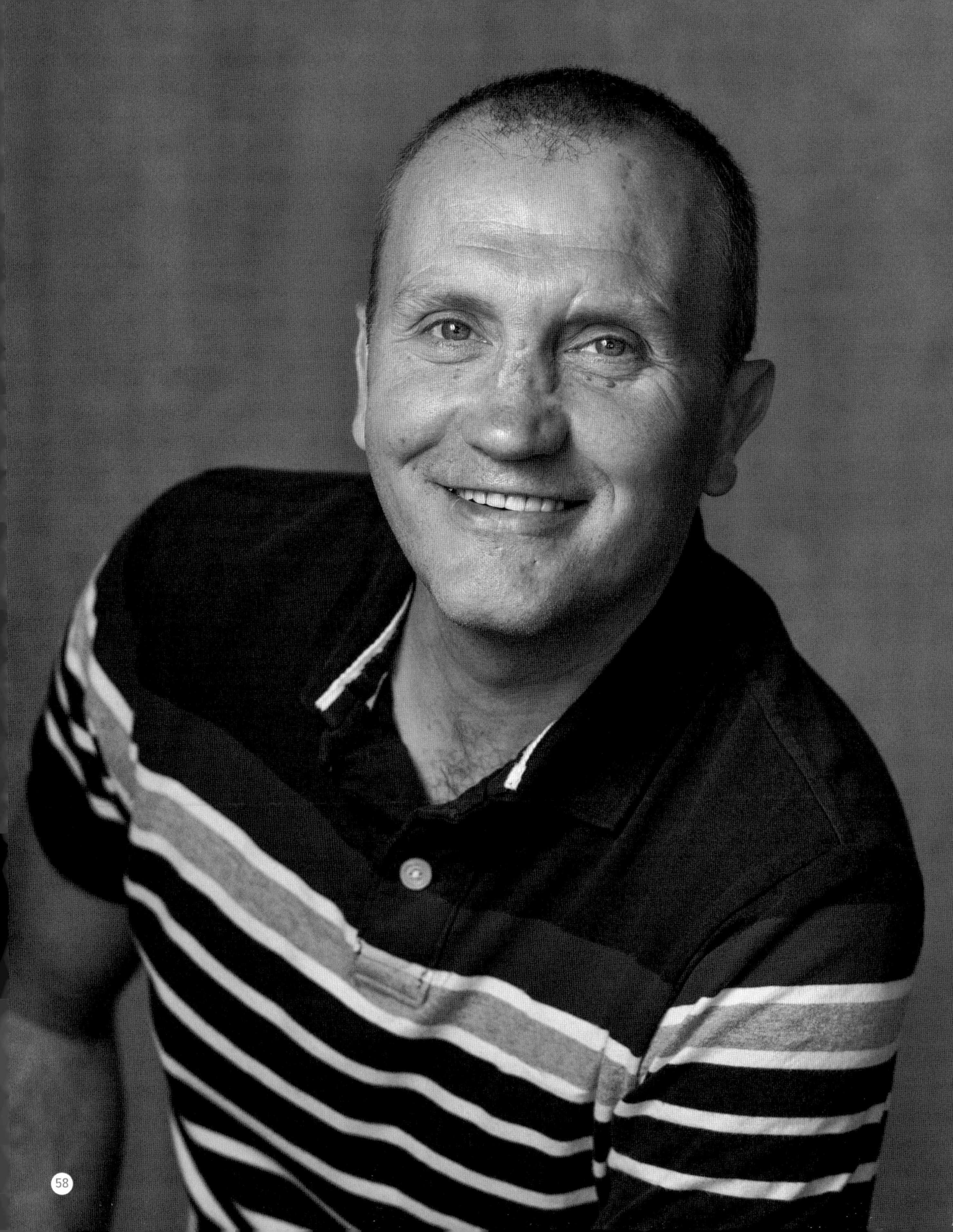

PETE

Liverpool

"Nothing helped or changed me, I was trapped: enslaved to my addictions."

From 12 to 38 years of age, Pete lived a life of addiction. Fourteen years of that time he spent with a partner and had two children. She also was a recreational drug user so his habits didn't change with the addition of the children. Once their relationship ended, he didn't know how to deal with the loss of his young children and a deep sadness filled him. "Some nights I slept rolled up in a carpet in a dumpster bin. I'd try to cry but there were no tears anymore. I'd have this picture of my kids asking their mom, 'Where is my dad?!'"

Even though Pete was living on the streets only eight miles from his family and six miles from his children, they had no idea where he was for four years. Sleeping in a dumpster bin one day, he awoke to the sound of the truck coming to empty the bin. He quickly rolled out of the side to escape being dumped or tipped out only to look up into the face of his sister! This was the start of finding real hope and change for Pete. He was introduced to a community of men and women at Betel who knew how to help him.

A few weeks later Pete was asked by his leader in the community, "Do you believe you'll ever see your children again?" His answer was an emotional, "I don't know." The leader replied with something Pete had never heard and didn't understand without explanation. "You need to believe because Jesus loves you and God will restore the things you've lost." A hope began to rise up in Pete for the first time.

After writing a flowery letter filled with lies to his kids, Pete ripped it up. His second attempt had true words in it like: drug addict, alcoholic, lost, broken, and homeless. He thought, "I can't send that to my little kids!" But yet, he knew God said do it. The next ten weeks were filled with a slow deflating of hope for Pete. One day, though, he received a large brown envelope with DADDY written across it. Inside was the most beautiful letter from his kids who hadn't seen him for over four years. The most valuable part was at the end which read, "P.S., Daddy we forgive you."

Today, Pete and his wife Dawn bring hope to other men who are going through the same pain he did. He doesn't patronize them with platitudes. Instead he helps them carry on, waiting for God to build bridges. "God enabled me to preach His word and took me from the bin to the pulpit."

"P.S., Daddy we forgive you."

DAWN

Northamptonshire

"I was such an insecure girl, no confidence. I was crushed by men, life and addiction. I was horrible on the inside and out, seeking love and needing a drink to give me what I needed."

Going to big, fancy parties at family friends' homes as a seven-year-old, Dawn started drinking alcohol. She liked the way it made her feel free and confident as a shy little girl. At 13, she sought love in a man, so her journey of seeking began. Sadly it took her down an unplanned and painful path. Being raped at 14 and again at 18 didn't deter her from looking for love among the men around her.

Being a professional ballet dancer took her many places and into many relationships. Alcohol, by this time, had become the love of her life because it gave her courage and confidence. "It became everything I needed to help me be who I thought I should be."

Later, due to an injury, she lost her dancing career and drinking took over her life. After three bottles of vodka a day she often would black out. None of the rehab places helped, in fact, she was banned from some of the centers.

One day she drank the last of her vodka, took her four-year-old son by the hand and trundled off in a drunken stupor to St. Peter's church. The vicar and a woman named Yvonne invested love into Dawn for the ensuing years. The power of their prayers wasn't fully realized till much later. Their prayers helped direct her to Betel where she found the perfect love she had always been seeking.

Dawn told me that two weeks after she chose to follow Jesus, she was riding down the road and suddenly saw the most beautiful color bursting towards her. "I've never seen such yellow. A massive amount of dandelion flowers! I never saw so many together in one place. I really felt the love of Jesus in that sight."

Perhaps this was bizarre but the color was astounding to her. A dandelion was a weed that everyone wanted to get rid of and Dawn identified with it. She thought, "How many people saw me as that weed that just needed (to be) pulled out, stamped on and poisoned to destroy it. But God created dandelions just like He created me and loves me." It was a profound and meaningful experience for her.

"God turned all of the addictions and pain around, He completely wooed me. It's His love that sustains me every day. I am secure in His love, who I am in Him. I am accepted. I went from someone who craved love, to having an abundance of love to give to others around me–God's love."

I went from someone who craved love, to having an abundance of love to give to others around me—God's love."

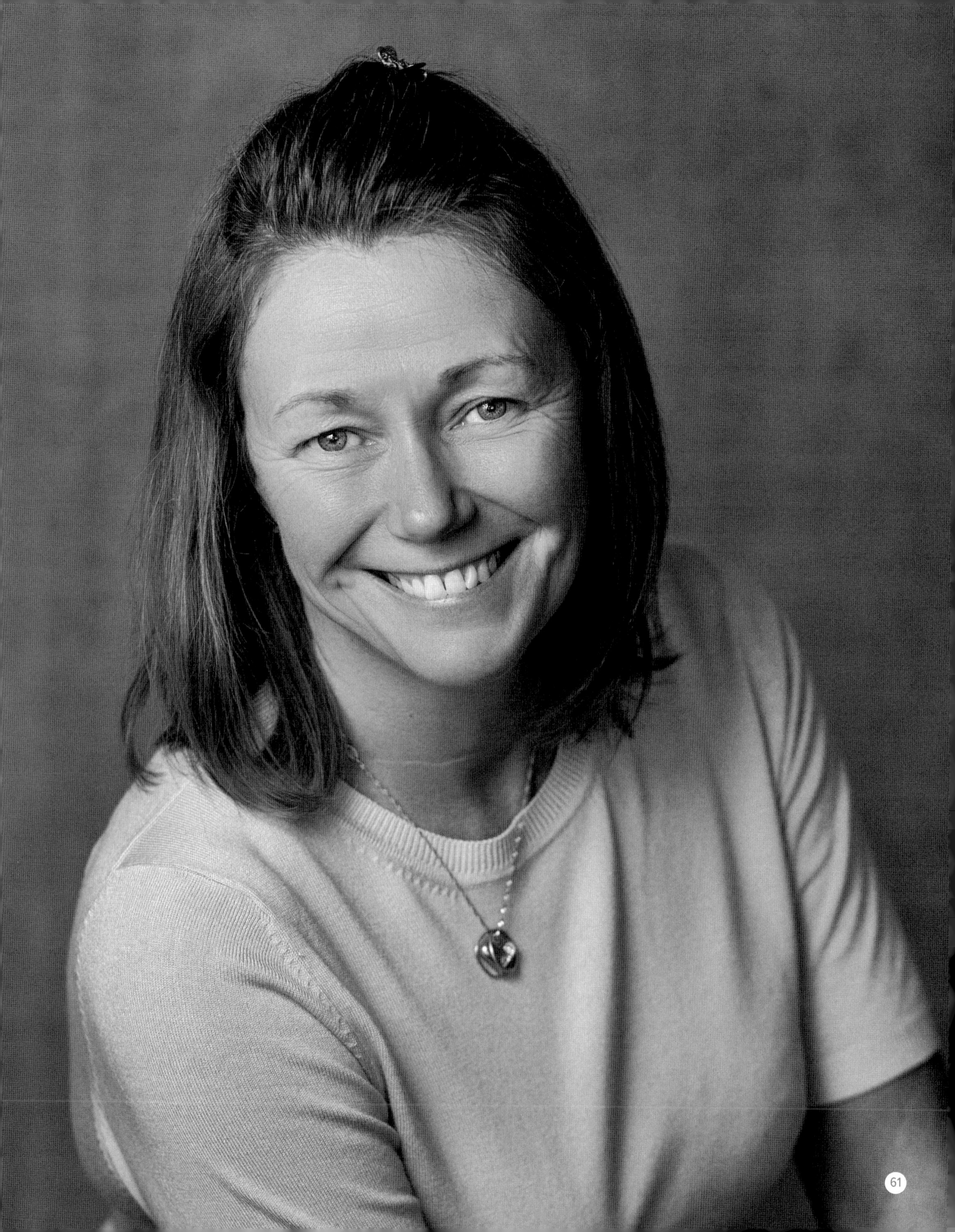

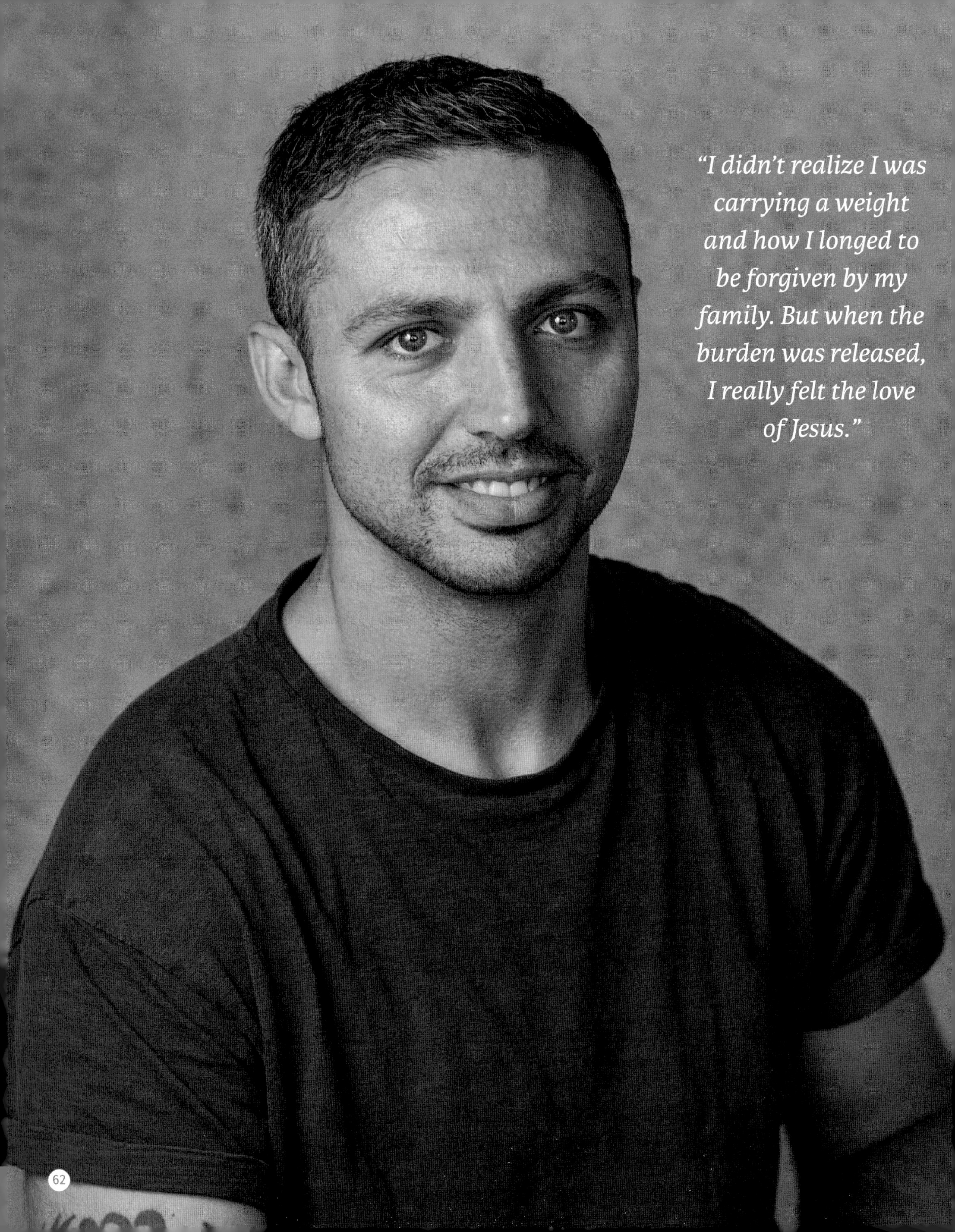

"I didn't realize I was carrying a weight and how I longed to be forgiven by my family. But when the burden was released, I really felt the love of Jesus."

RICKY

Essex

"I decided that my life would probably be over in the next six months. It wasn't that I was trying to die but I just didn't care if I did. I didn't see a future. I didn't see a way off the carousel–this dodgy merry-go-round."

Ricky grew up thinking God was a fairy tale for people outside of the estates (government housing). He thought, "If God was real, why would He let all this [poverty] go on around him." By 12 years old, he was selling enough cannabis to smoke for free. Losing his granddad and father within a year of each other gave him an excuse to go more extreme with drug abuse. After an accident at work in which he almost lost the lower half of his leg, he dove into heroin use. The next nine years he had well-paying jobs but also used drugs constantly, overdosing some 30 times. Even dying on three separate occasions and being brought back to life didn't change the course of his life. He tells of how ungrateful he was to the paramedic who gave him the blocker drug and saved his life with a defibrillator. "I demanded to be let out of the ambulance!"

Within one month, Ricky went from living in a three-bedroom home to living in a tent in Epping Forest. Arriving home to his campsite one day, he found that someone had stolen his tent, his chairs, his homemade stove and his bedding. Everything was gone.

Ricky began going to a night shelter where there was a strict no tolerance policy regarding drugs. However, one night as he was sitting in the church bathroom with a needle in his arm, like he did every night, God broke into his life. He found himself in tears asking, "Is this all I can expect from life?" And he heard God say to his heart, "No! Tell Stan (shelter leader) what you are doing." He immediately thought, "No way, I'll be banned from all the shelters." But for some reason, he felt reassured that it would be okay.

Stan referred Ricky to Betel where it turned out to be more than okay. It was the start of a new life for him. A homeless thief and functional addict for many years, Ricky soon found himself living in a replica castle—serving in Betel Melbourne, Australia. He became a leader of a house of Betel guys, organizing garden jobs and doing job quotes. On top of that he had the responsibility of carrying a credit card with a $10,000 limit on it, where before he couldn't be responsible for $10. "I was so grateful for life and how Jesus brought me further than I ever thought possible."

Family relationships had been stretched while he lived in addiction. But after apologizing to his family for his behavior, Ricky broke down in tears. He couldn't control himself. He told me, "I didn't realize I was carrying a weight and how I longed to be forgiven by my family. But when the burden was released, I really felt the love of Jesus."

SARA

Barking

"I cried every night but I didn't have the courage to tell anybody. I didn't want to be bullied any more. I wanted these people to want me and like me, so I kept quiet." At eleven, Sara found an opportunity to buy the acceptance of the group that was bullying her. But after being dared to drink alcohol with these kids, they left her alone at the skate park, passed out. She woke up to find a much older man beside her. He raped her. "Afterwards he told me that if I said anything, he would tell everybody that it was all my idea and that I had asked for it. I believed him."

Sara became increasingly angry. "I no longer had to worry about bullies because I became one." Alcohol and weed became a way to cover up her feelings. Kicked out of school and her home, she became even more violent—being arrested three times a week became normal. It always took several officers to restrain her. In and out of mental hospitals, numerous therapists and rehabs only made her angrier. Suicide attempts were met with doctors giving her more pills to hold her over until she could get help. "I was already in self-destruct mode and nothing could stop me."

Finding Jesus through Betel was the only path to freedom for Sara. "The peace I now have is unshakeable. No one can ever take it away." Being raped had stolen so much from Sara. She kept that experience a secret for 14 years. Sara didn't believe she could be healed from the pain or that freedom from it was possible. "It had been kept in the dark for so long, I thought it was always going to be dark, but as soon as I spoke about it, it became a little bit lighter. You expect people to judge you or to pity you. But the best thing anyone can do is just listen. That is the most beautiful thing anyone can do."

As a believer in Jesus she has really struggled with the question, "If God was there for me why did that happen? Where the heck was He? It's been hard for me to see Him in that position (watching over her); I've never been able to see Him there, ever." But recently God gave Sara an exceptional insight-inspired picture in her mind of Him being with her in that moment, drowning out the voice of the abuser. She told me, "I felt powerful, like, you don't have a hold on me, you can't get me anymore." Healing has been beautiful for Sara. She says that Jesus has empowered her and she now is able to help and encourage other women who have experienced the same things she did.

"I realized that His love for me was irrevocable, no matter what. I felt so secure for the first time in my life. God's goodness is boundless, relentless, and it desires all of us."

"The peace I now have is unshakeable. No one can ever take it away."

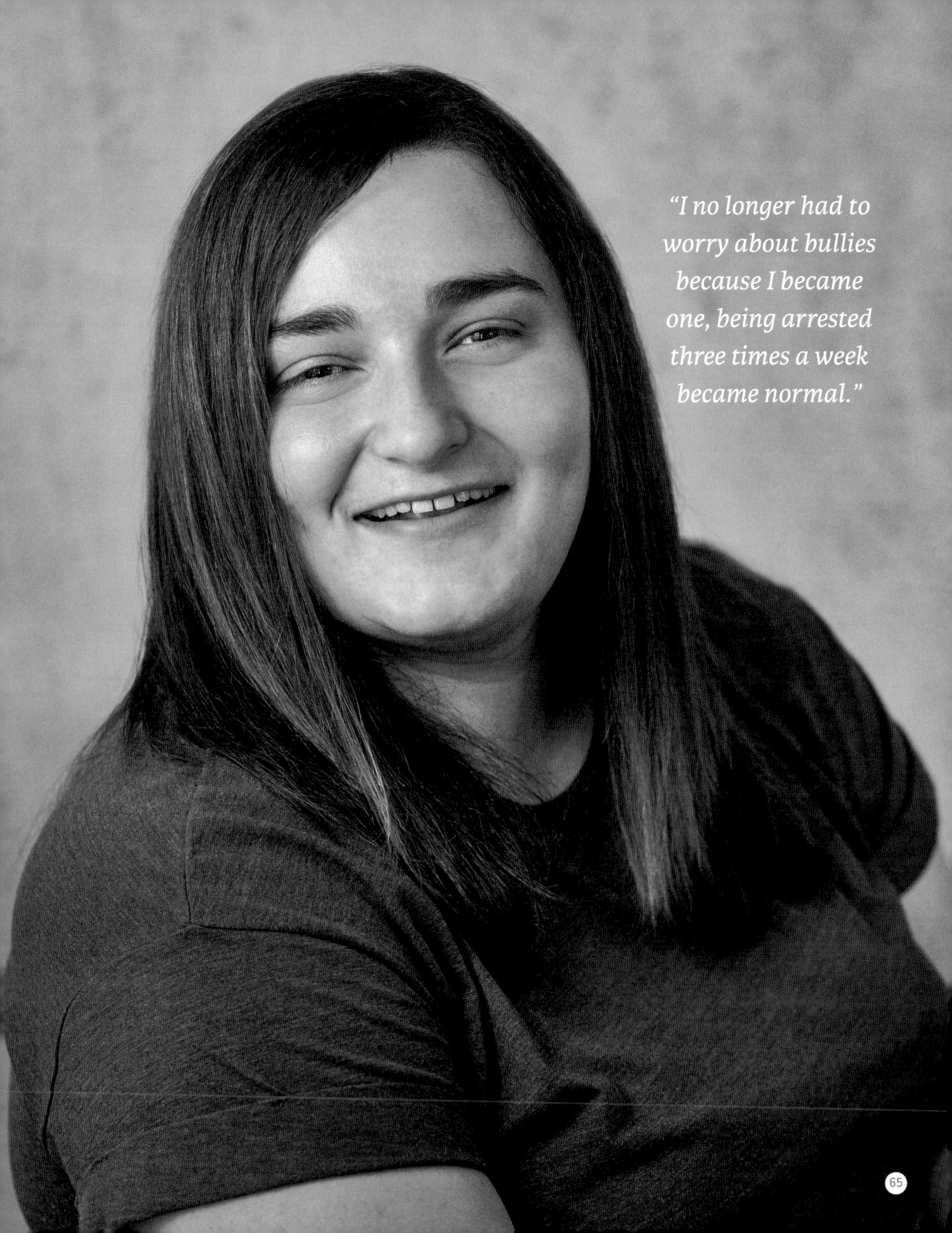

"I no longer had to worry about bullies because I became one, being arrested three times a week became normal."

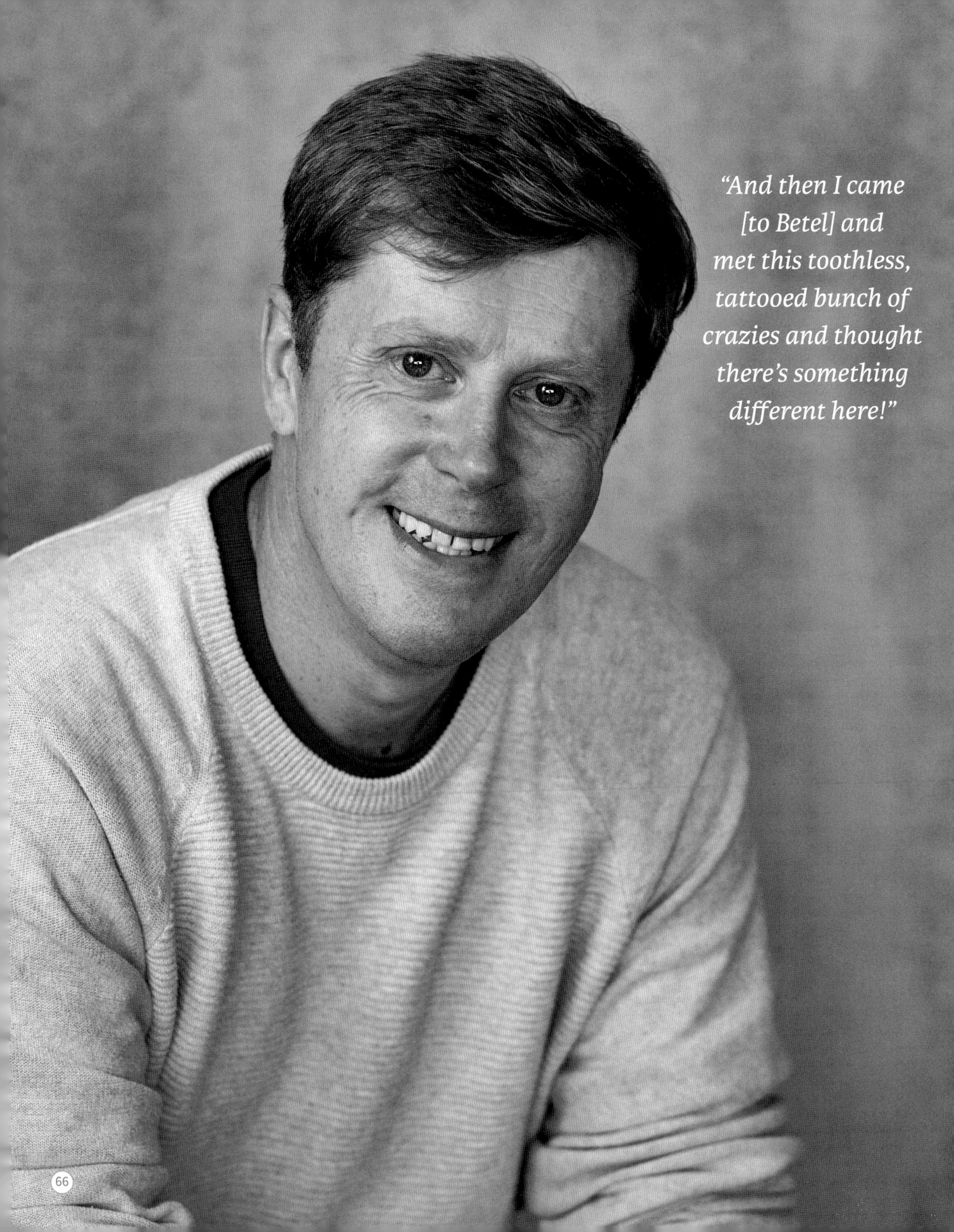

"And then I came [to Betel] and met this toothless, tattooed bunch of crazies and thought there's something different here!"

LUKE

South Wales

Luke spent 23 years burdened by addictions. He used heroin, with breaks of alcohol and other pharmaceutical drugs. He told of a certain Thursday morning that changed everything for him. He was going out of his mind, curled up in a ball and silently wishing to die. He had just talked to his mom with the intention of getting money from her for drugs. This time she wouldn't let her fear of him taking his own life manipulate her. Here's the story in his own words:

"I don't know if you've ever stared at a digital clock for a full minute—let alone for 45 in complete silence—it was torture. I paced while silently staring, waiting and watching the minutes change.

BUZZ! The electric shock of the downstairs door bell jolted me. I buzzed her in and my skin turned electric. Every hair stood to attention. I felt both excited and sick at the same time. I heard her footsteps behind the door. I quickly glanced over the state of my life but I was past caring. Everything was upside down.

This was the first time I'd truly exposed the depth of my addiction to her. How would she respond? But it was too late; she was the only one who could help me.

As I opened the heavy door, I cowered like Gollum shrinking back, but it was just her. She was alone but there was an unexplained bright light with her and it made something inside of me feel uneasy, unsettled, like it didn't belong.

She entered my hell and looked at me with light burning inside her eyes. As she said, "LUKE," I heard an authority and anger in Mum's voice I'd never heard before.

Then the burning light, became a raging fire, then turned to a warming compassion. In that moment, with all my weakness, my brokenness, my desperation and despair something inside me shifted, from hopeless to hopeful."

That Thursday Luke's mom brought the light of Jesus and a plan to go to Betel. Luke's plan was to come into Betel and get off the needles so he could go back and smoke drugs. "I thought I'd come in and meet loads of Ned Flanders[1] kind of Christian characters. I'd be great, I could manipulate them for two weeks, and get some train fare home and smoke drugs. And then I came [to Betel] and met this toothless, tattooed bunch of crazies and thought 'there's something different here!'"

Many years later, now a leader at Betel with his wife, Luke shared, "I'd always been addicted, it was who I was. It was my full identity and nothing was going to ever change it. Except God, and only God, had a different path. God had a different purpose for me and my life. That long ago morning, Jesus Christ came to save me from my hell. Today I stand healed, redeemed, with a new identity as a co-heir with Christ. I am free." God now works together with Luke to speak life and encouragement to hundreds of people recovering each year.

[1]Ned Flanders is an extremely religious, good-natured, cheery, pushover next-door neighbor on "The Simpsons" television show.

CHARLES

Nigeria, Africa

At midnight Charles and his friends were on their way to Waterloo in London to buy cheap alcohol. It was a thirty-minute trip he took almost daily. But this time he changed his mind and decided to go to a club instead. His five friends went on ahead. They met a drunk, middle-aged man on Hungerford Bridge and decided he would be easy to mug. However, a simple theft turned into murder when he put up a fight and ended up being thrown into the Thames River by the four guys and one young girl. All of them went to prison or to mental institutions. Charles thought, "I escaped that one!" He felt invincible and lucky. Instead of this being a wakeup call for his dangerous lifestyle, he kept going.

"I sank deeper into my crack addiction and every immoral act that came with it. I lived in depravity; everything I had or touched, including people, were corrupted."

After more than 20 years of addiction to alcohol, crack and heroin, Charles lost his flat (apartment) because he used it as a dealer den and a brothel. An altercation with a drug dealer caused him to hide in a trash bin shed for five days until he was terribly sick from withdrawal. He decided to find help.

Charles found it at Betel and was overwhelmed by the feeling and atmosphere of peace he experienced. Being surrounded by others who truly knew what he was going through as he suffered withdraws encouraged him to keep going.

Charles stated, "I very quickly kicked my addiction but began to realize the emptiness of my heart. I needed to fill a massive void in my life; going back to my old life was not an option." He had tasted the realness of Jesus and it caused a craving for more. Charles once was lost in a world of crime, drugs and violence but now he has found a life of peace and joy. He leads others to this peace as well as managing a furniture restoration business in Derby. Charles says, "God's love is evident in every single thing that I do. It's a daily experience to see lives changed."

"I sank deeper into my crack addiction and every immoral act that came with it. I lived in depravity; everything I had or touched was corrupted."

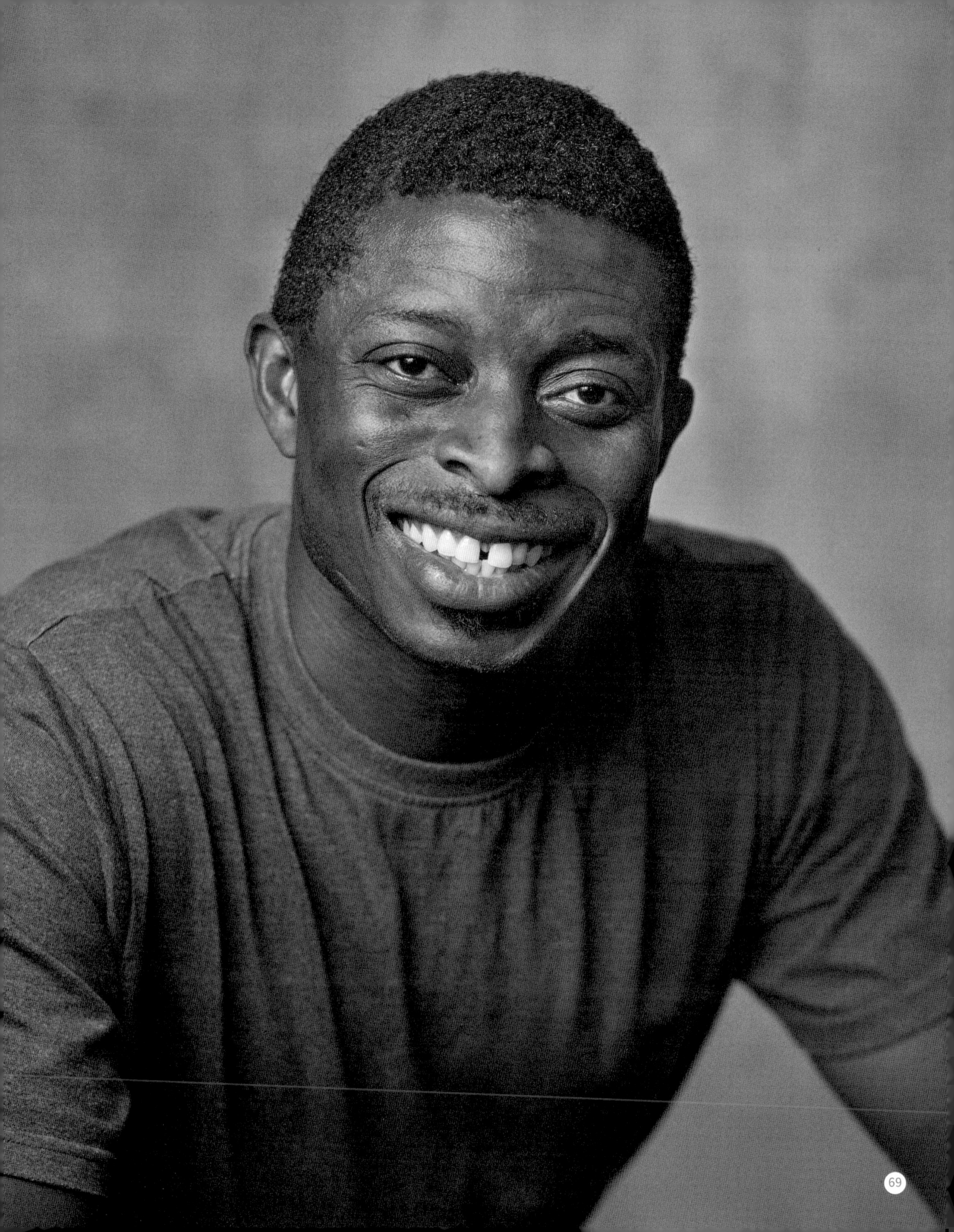

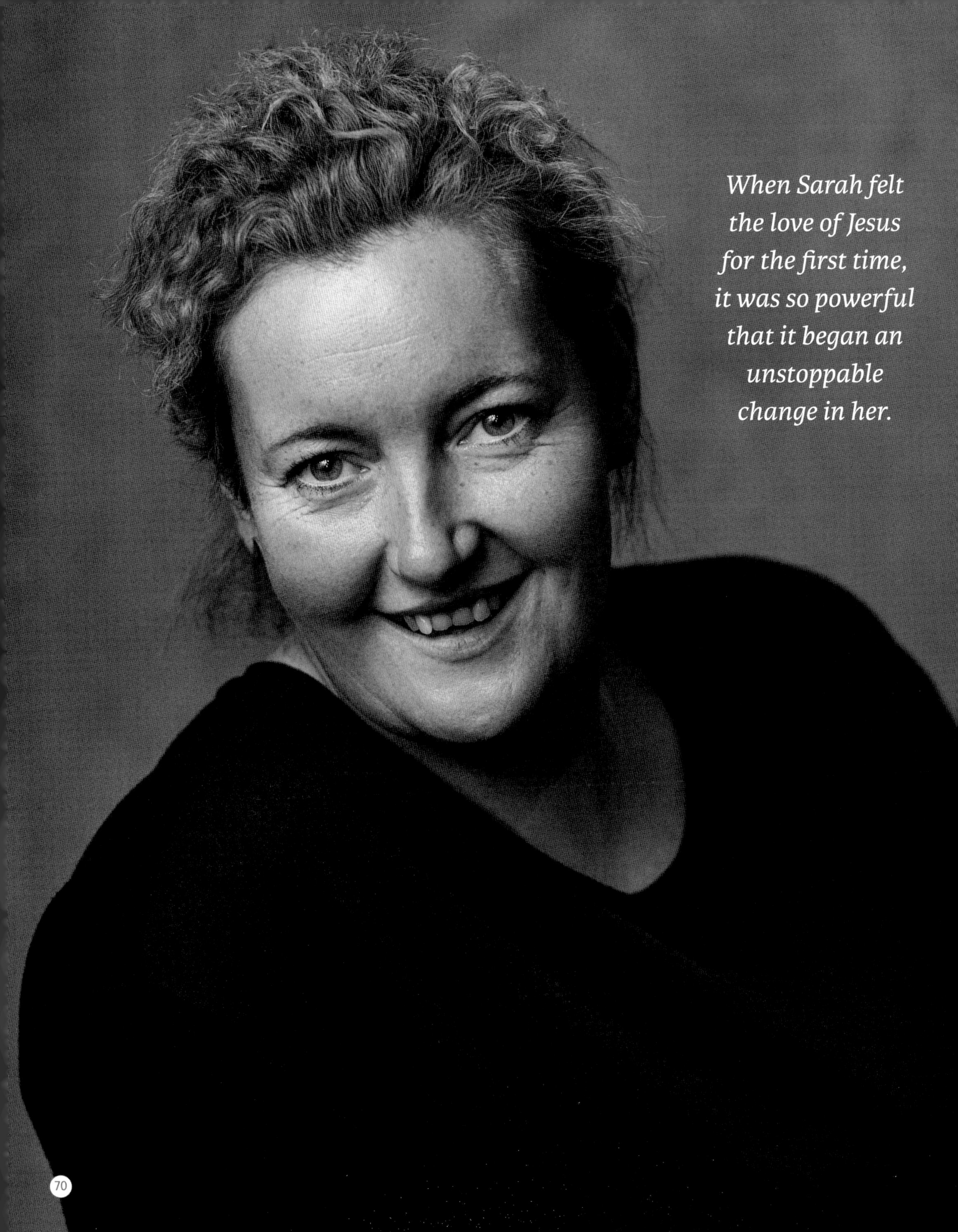

When Sarah felt the love of Jesus for the first time, it was so powerful that it began an unstoppable change in her.

SARAH

Wales

Sarah had never felt love before in her life. She had no clue what it felt like to be loved or accepted in any way. Her whole life, from birth, was one of rejection, abuse and extreme violence. Sarah left her abusive home at age 14, which began a life of prostitution and drug addiction. Violence was very much a part of her life working on the streets. The only breaks she would have were short stays in a hospital after getting beaten up or psych evaluations in the psychiatric ward.

In and out of rehabs for various time periods, she always went back to the streets. "That was all I knew; it was my job." She met a guy who was in a gang and started a relationship with him. He was into "really sick, disgusting, vile stuff" as were the other gang members. She ended up getting stabbed and almost lost her arm. Rushed to the hospital, she prayed that God would save her arm, and He did.

At that same time, she was pregnant without knowing it. It was a miracle that the baby survived because Sarah had bruises all over her body, even foot marks where this man would kick her. Her mental anguish was so extreme that she had been diagnosed with many different disorders, including multiple personality disorder.

When Sarah felt the love of Jesus for the first time, it was so powerful that it began an unstoppable change in her. Currently, Sarah says of herself, "I'm completely different now." After a short time in Betel, she was praying in a worship service. As she closed her eyes, a warm feeling came upon her head and slid down to her toes, filling her. She suddenly burst into tears. These tears were a really big relief for Sarah because as she said, "I didn't cry. I did not do it. It was a weakness to me. But I just felt so secure. So loved. So safe!"

Today, Sarah doesn't struggle with mental disorders; once she got off drugs and began the healing process, the mental disorders fell away. She is living and working at Betel and has a growing relationship with her daughter.

ROBERT

Hartlepool

Robert and his brothers seemed to always be in trouble with the law from an early age. The police were at his home often. He easily followed in his older brother's footsteps. Later on, his older brother, Roy, left the life of crime and found faith in Jesus. But for Robert, drugs, crime and alcohol took over his entire life. At one point, he even moved in with Roy and chose to believe in Jesus but couldn't get off drugs.

Later on, heroin caused even more destruction in Robert's life. Being in prison many times didn't change his path. He had three children he could never see, lost a brother to drugs and then his sister as well. Everything was out of control in his life. However, he did end up taking care of the only rock in his life, his mom, as she died of cancer. On her death bed she gave her forgiveness for all Robert had done and shared her dying wish. She wished she could have seen him clean. But he couldn't give her that.

Robert was kicked out of the family home after his mom's death and he had nowhere to go. He slept in a newspaper skip. It was through a local church that he found a home at Betel. The hardest part for him was the first four weeks because he didn't sleep at all while he came off methadone. He made it through and his healing process began. "God started to break addiction, depression, and hurt from my life. I found a love that never gives up."

After sharing his story one day, his friend responded with, "That's a shame, because you are actually a good guy." Robert hadn't heard anything positive about himself for many years. God used this kind word to open his eyes and cause him to re-evaluate how he thought of himself. He said, "I felt I was released from so much of the past." Who Robert was created to be had been hidden from him and now was being revealed.

Many years earlier he had tried giving his life to Jesus but he still lacked power to make real change in his life. He encountered the love of Jesus in a fresh way and realized it was more than words that save. This is how he explained it, "Believing in Jesus is more than just a salvation prayer—it's following. Although I said it with my mouth, I wasn't actually following."

In recent years Robert has seen many members of his family restored to him and he has been released from mountains of pain and suffering. He shared, "I was nearly dead but now I'm alive! Jesus restored my mind and equipped me to stand firm."

"God started to break addiction, depression, and hurt from my life. I found a love that never gives up."

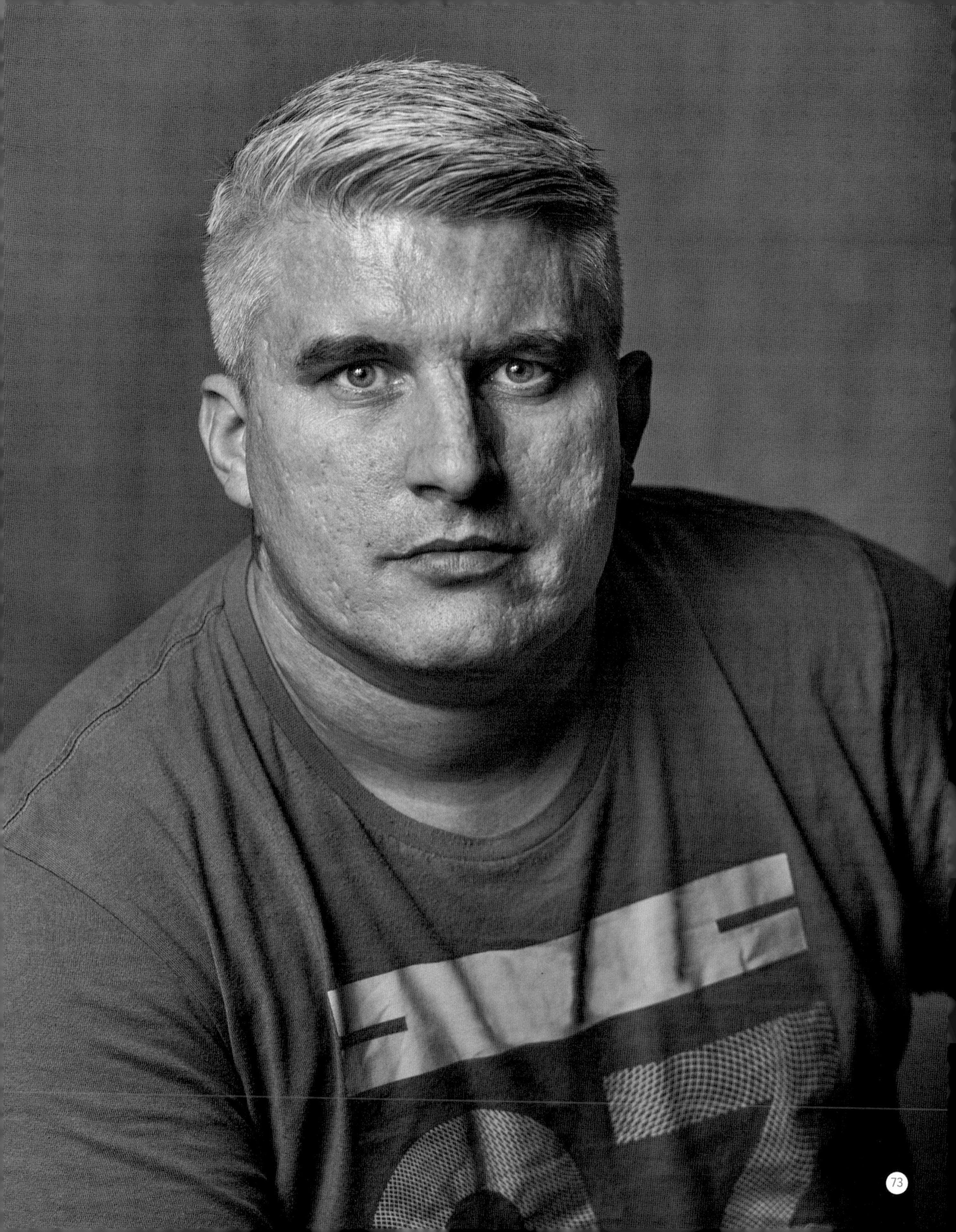

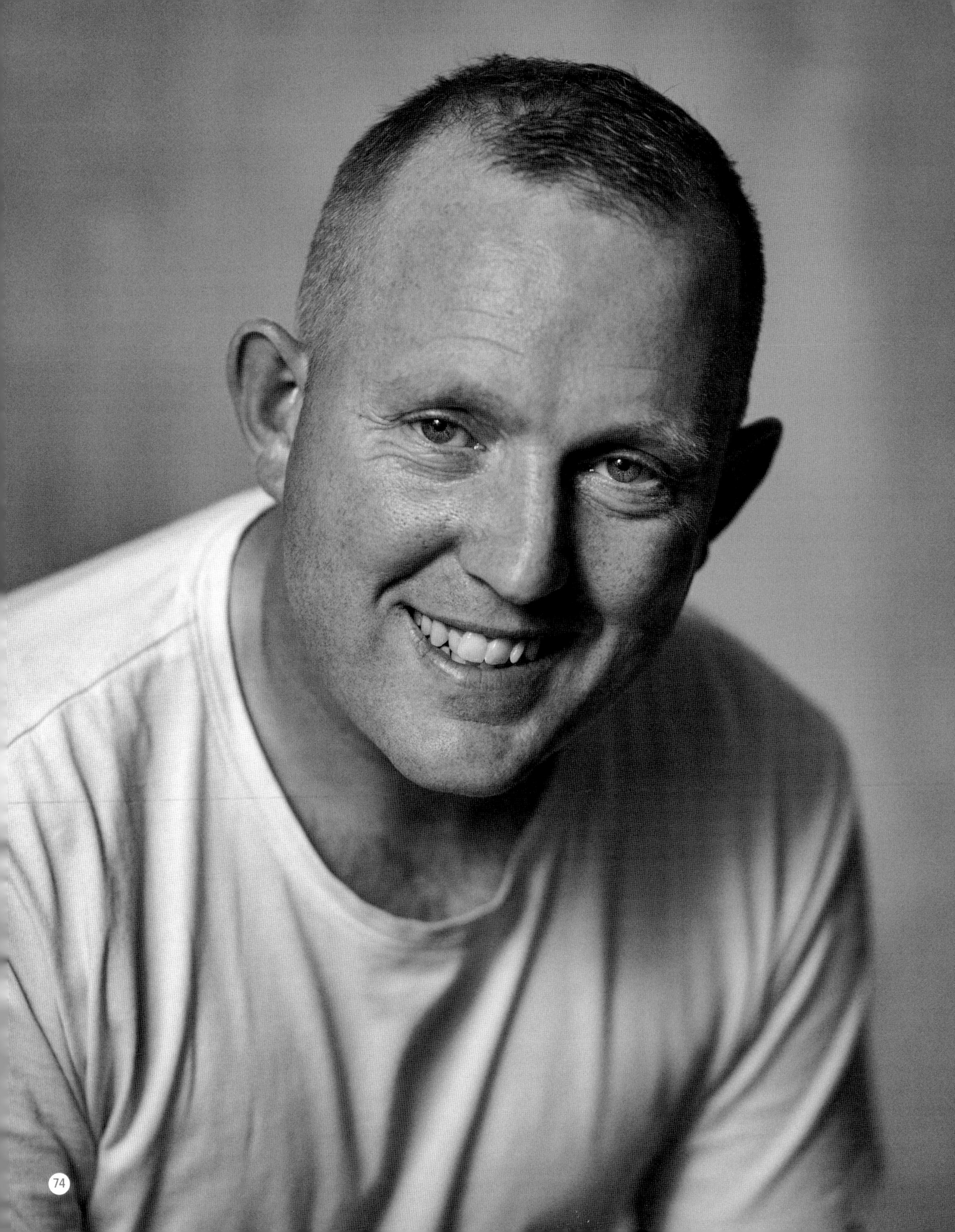

DAVID

Nottingham

For seven years David lived with an addiction to drugs—specifically heroin. His main belief about himself during this time was, "This is me, a wasteful drug addict." All through the loneliness and hopelessness he said he did have a small sense that there was a God but he didn't know how to believe. "What is faith? What is the purpose of this life?" were always the questions in the back of his mind. Towards the end of the seven years, David made the final decision to try and change his life. He was now at his parents' house, and in desperation he prayed to God for strength and deliverance. And something unexplainable happened to him. He felt as if he was free from the addiction.

The usual withdrawals and anxieties that come with detoxing were not kicking in like they had other times. David's older brother was suspicious of his new-found freedom from addiction. He thought David was faking it to win favor from his parents. So to test David, his brother gave him naltrexone[1] which can instantly detox a person from heroin. But nothing happened since heroin wasn't in his system anymore! David also wanted to test himself so he went to get some more drugs at a friend's house where others was getting high on heroin and crack. They refused to give him anything. David said he began to see that God was real and had saved him from certain death. He began glimpsing hope for a purposeful life and to ask, "How can I serve this God?"

David has now been free from addiction for nearly twenty years. Together with his wife, he serves as pastor and regional director of Betel in North East England.

This is what David believes now: "Some say, 'always an alcoholic, always an addict.' But that is rubbish! You can be totally set free. I contradict all the professionals as I'm totally set free from addiction. I don't even think about it. I could go anywhere now."

[1]Naltrexone belongs to a class of drugs known as opiate antagonists. It works in the brain to prevent opiate effects (e.g., feelings of well-being, pain relief). It also decreases the desire to take opiates.

AUSTIN

Hartford

"I woke up in a bus stop one morning, I had the clothes on my back, some vodka and a few tablets of drugs. I lay there watching the rain pouring down and thought, 'Something is wrong with this picture.'" Austin realized after 20 years of violence, anger, and bitterness fueled by drugs and alcohol he was killing himself.

As a young man of 22, his life dramatically changed from happy to torment. He and his pregnant wife watched as their 22-month-old daughter died from meningitis just nine hours after being diagnosed. The stress of it all created strain on her pregnancy which almost caused them to lose their second daughter as well.

To cope with this great loss, Austin began drinking. When that wasn't enough to numb the pain, he took any tablets he could get his hands on. His plan was to be totally alone. "In my world, if I was alone, I didn't have anyone close to me, I couldn't get hurt." He accomplished his goal and lost everything; wife, children, family, job, and home. He ended up on the streets, eating out of a dumpster behind McDonald's.

There was only one person in the whole world who wouldn't let go of Austin; a pastor who was relentless in pursuing him. This is who Austin turned to after that day in the bus stop. It wasn't until he was in the hospital from alcohol-induced seizures that he discovered the truth about his real problem. He said, "I realized that [the problem with my life] wasn't the drugs or the alcohol, it was the person I had become because when I fueled the anger and bitterness with drugs and alcohol it would come out as a rage. There was a lot of violence!"

When he arrived at Betel he noticed the men there had something he didn't have. He didn't know exactly what it was but he decided he wanted it. One prayer changed everything. There was no fanfare, no fireworks, just a prayer. Looking back, something changed with that specific prayer and afterward he was receptive to Jesus, starting a difficult but amazing process. Now he has a relationship with his children and family and is using those 20 years of chaos for some good to help guys in similar brokenness find freedom and restoration.

Never underestimate the quietness of one prayer. Austin says he remembers that one prayer like it was yesterday and says, "God has done some amazing things."

"I realized that...I fueled the anger and bitterness with drugs and alcohol—it would come out as rage—20 years of violence."

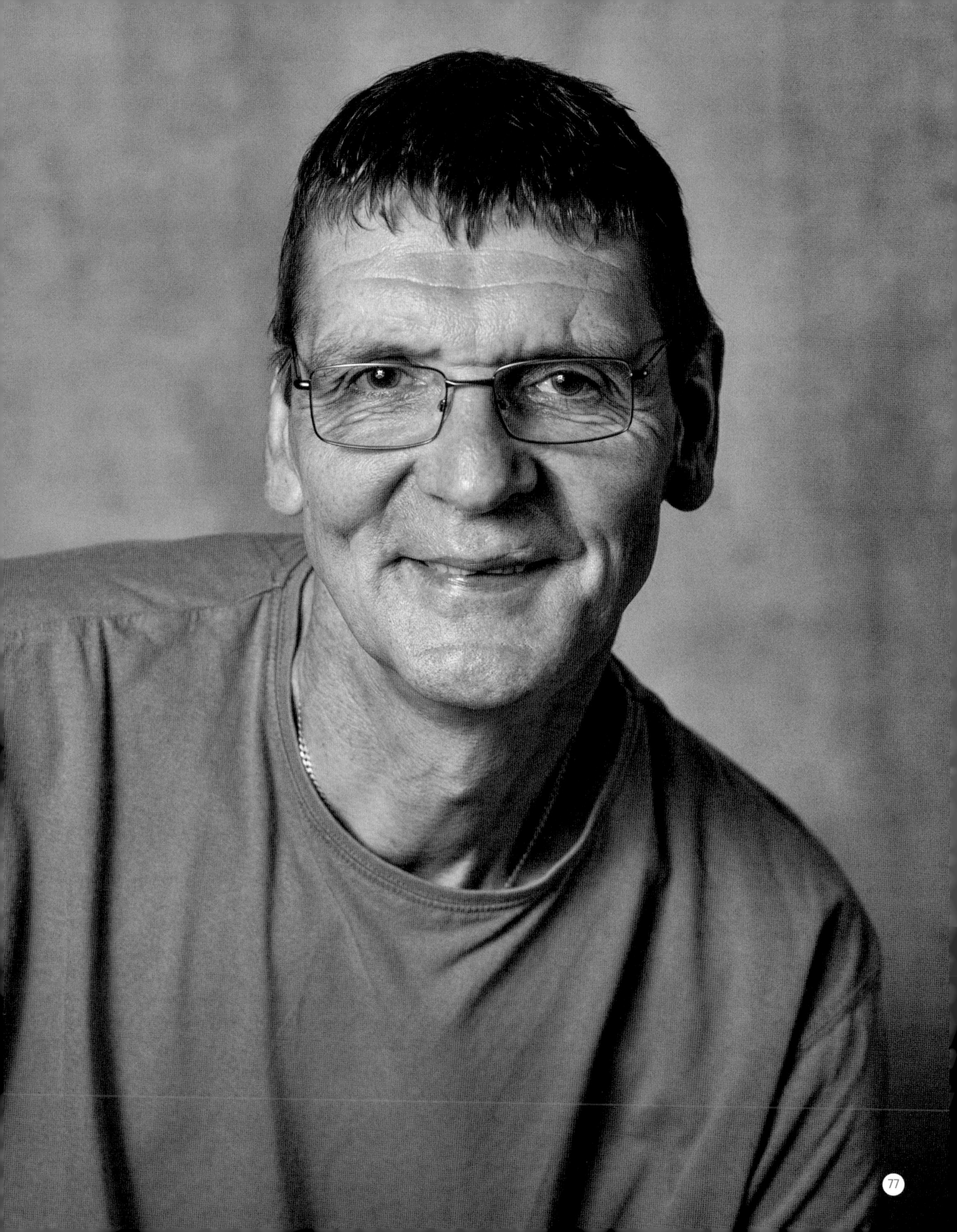

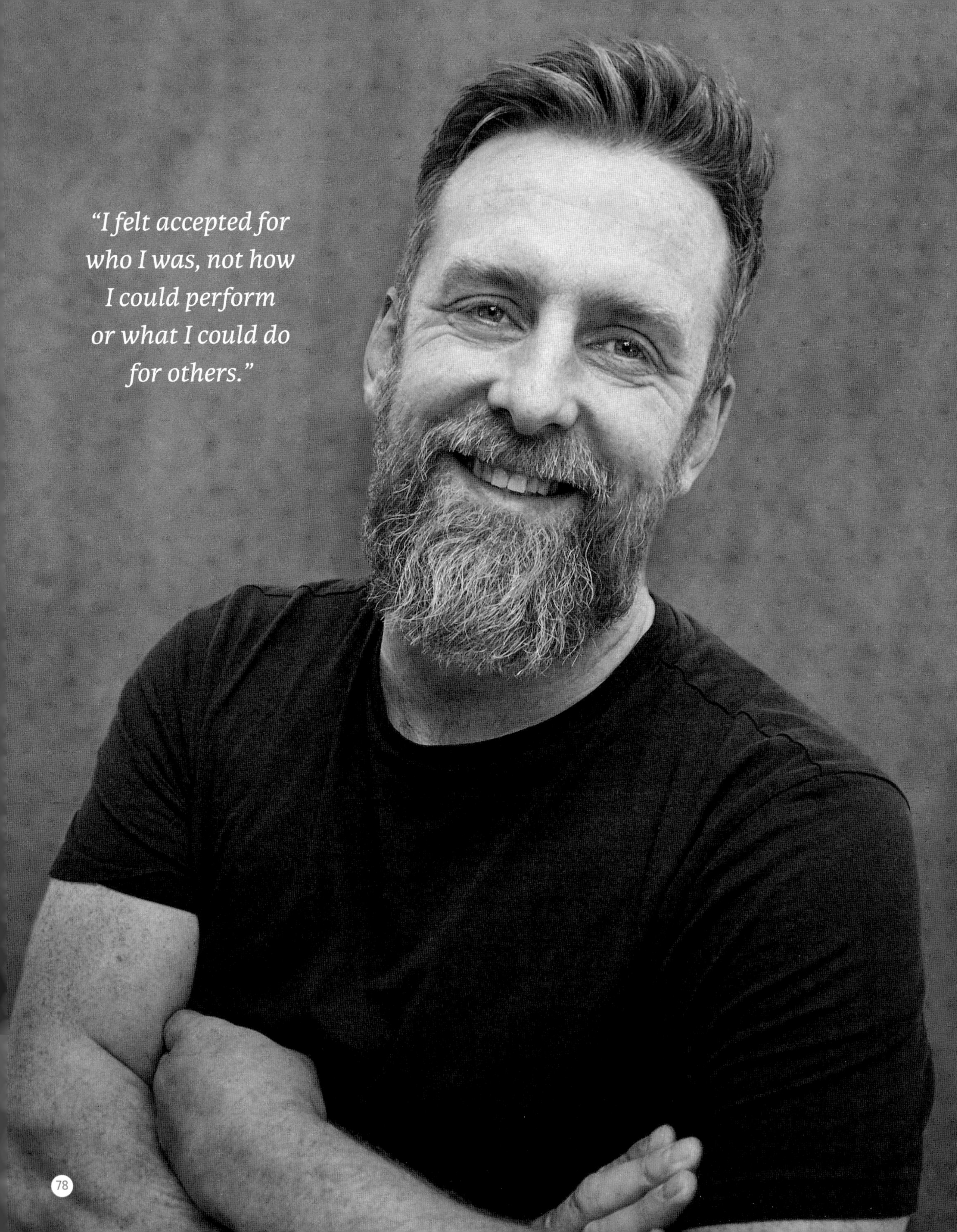

"I felt accepted for who I was, not how I could perform or what I could do for others."

PAUL

Kidderminster

"I can't do this anymore!" thought Paul as he watched the New Year's Eve festivities from the flat with no heat or electricity. He turned away and tried to end his life with a piece of glass laying on the floor. But he stopped short because as he put it, "I was too chicken to even do that." Paul instead took a walk and ended up at his old school. At the school's church he looked up at the steeple and said, "God if you are #%@&*$!# real, you need to show yourself, because I'm stuck and I can't get out!"

Six years earlier, Paul had started smoking cannabis, taking ecstasy and speed. All he ever wanted was to be accepted and feel included. At five years old, he experienced rejection from school mates that wounded his heart deeply. That experience drove Paul to perform for acceptance. At fifteen, to prove he was tougher and better than others, he would take ten ecstasy pills when everyone else was just taking one.

He smoked cannabis in such excess that he had cannabis-induced psychosis. He would see shadows following him and was paranoid of his best friends. Because of this, Paul started taking heroin. The heroin rid him of the paranoia and physical pain in his legs from his job. In a short time he sabotaged significant relationships, leaving him alone and rejected. For the next five years Paul lived in a cycle of: earn money, buy drugs, do drugs, repeat.

After he yelled at God in the chapel yard, life got worse for Paul. Drug dealers he owed money to beat him up daily and he was falsely accused of stealing. Paul told me, "I loved drugs!" He wanted to escape the violence and needed a change. He humbled himself and went home to ask his parents to take him into the countryside and drop him off, away from the town. His mom, whom he had stolen from many times, had compassion and called Betel.

Once at Betel, he survived the hallucinations and paranoia that came with cold turkey withdrawal, with the help of those who had experienced it before. Paul quickly felt like he belonged, what he had always longed for. He said, "I felt accepted for who I was, not how I could perform or what I could do for others."

Although Paul went in 'loving' drugs, within a few months of being at Betel he had a complete turnaround. He quickly accepted that the Bible was true and real. No one had ever shared the truth of Jesus with him. He said, "I never heard it. But when I first heard it, I knew it was true!" After realizing the truth he said, "I hated that old lifestyle. I hated drugs with a passion."

Paul has been at Betel for the past 20 years. Most of which, Paul and his wife along with their three children, have been pastors and directors at Betel Nottingham. When asked how he can sacrifice 20 years of his life he said, "It's not a sacrifice, it's an honor and a privilege which changes me from the inside out." Paul is an accomplished musician and luthier (guitar maker). "Creative" and "dynamic" describe Paul today.

As we talked about his story he told me, "When I look and remember where I came from, I still find it hard to believe that person was me. It seems so far away, it's like a story of another person's life. That pain and anguish is just like a distant memory that's been replaced by this amazing, unexplainable joy, hope and peace. I now have vision and purpose, relationships, friendships and great leaders that support me."

BRIAN

Scotland

Feeling betrayed by his parents' extramarital affairs, Brian led a life of addiction and crime. For 20 years he was in and out of jail and ruined all of his relationships. Things got so bad that he could only go out at night when he could hide in the shadows. This is when he finally sought help and found a home at Betel UK.

Over the years, the police had pressed charges many times for crimes Brian had committed, but it wasn't until he was *wrongly* accused of a crime that his faith in Jesus was solidified. This trial went on for weeks with false accusations and false witnesses. In the end, the evidence brought in proved false and all charges were dropped.

But the next scene was completely unexpected. The judge read to the court all of his outstanding charges and crimes, which were many. The judge then looked at Brian and said, "There is something absolutely different about you standing in front of me today. I've heard about all these Christian communities, but I see there is something completely different about you. And I believe that it is your will to go back there after this court case. Is that right?"

Brian replied, "Yes" and in his heart was thinking, "Betel is my home. It's my heart to help men get free of drug addiction like I truly never believed I could. But today I am free." The judge then smiled and to Brian's astonishment added, "You are exonerated of all charges."

Today Brian stands with no shame and guilt regarding his past; he is truly free to move forward in what he has been created to become. He has been set free not just by the court system but by God. Brian's excitement, in knowing that freedom is possible, fuels him to help others walk toward their liberation.

"God speaks to each of us differently in hopes that we will speak it out to the world," Brian says.

"God loved me first, even when I was very unlovable."

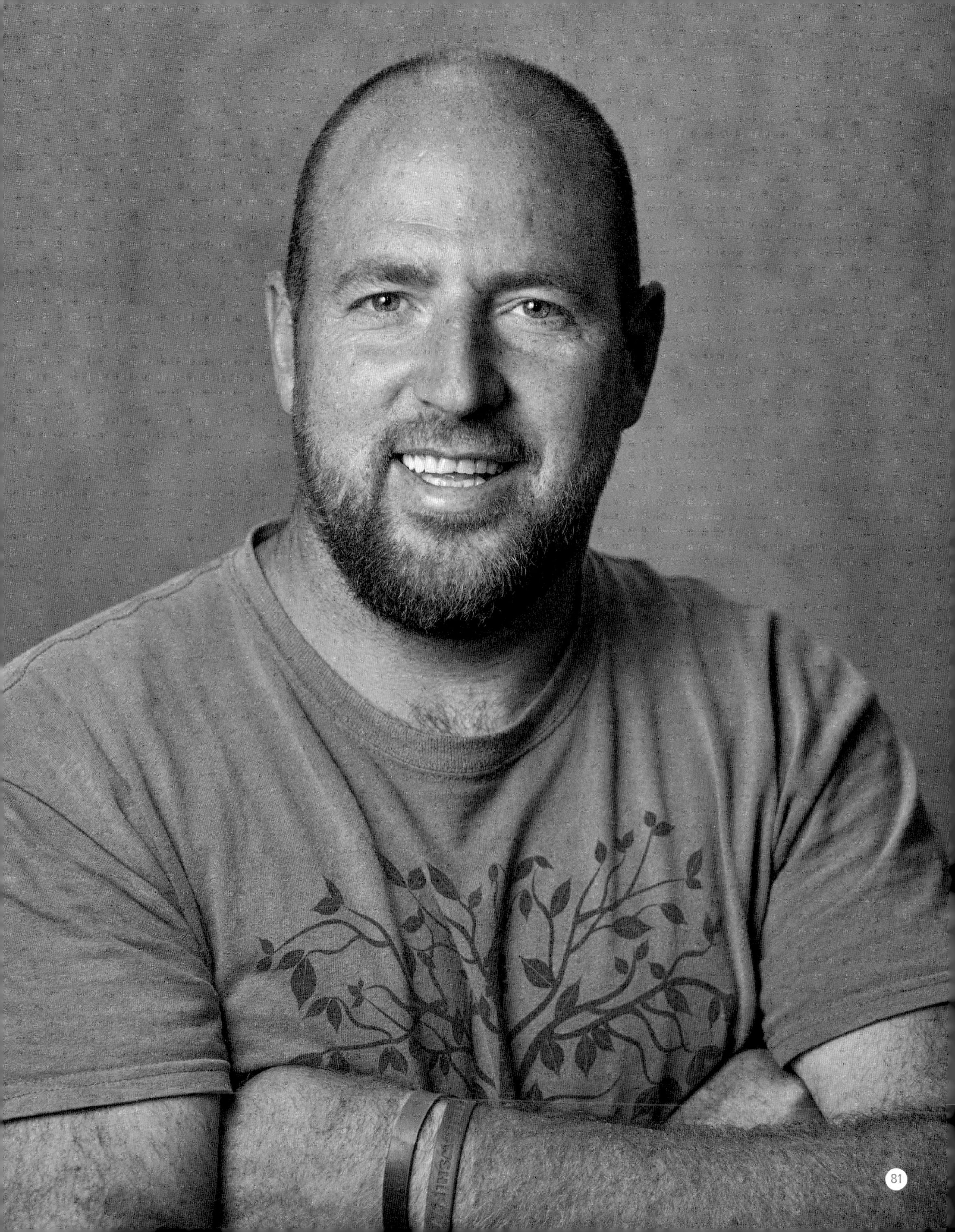

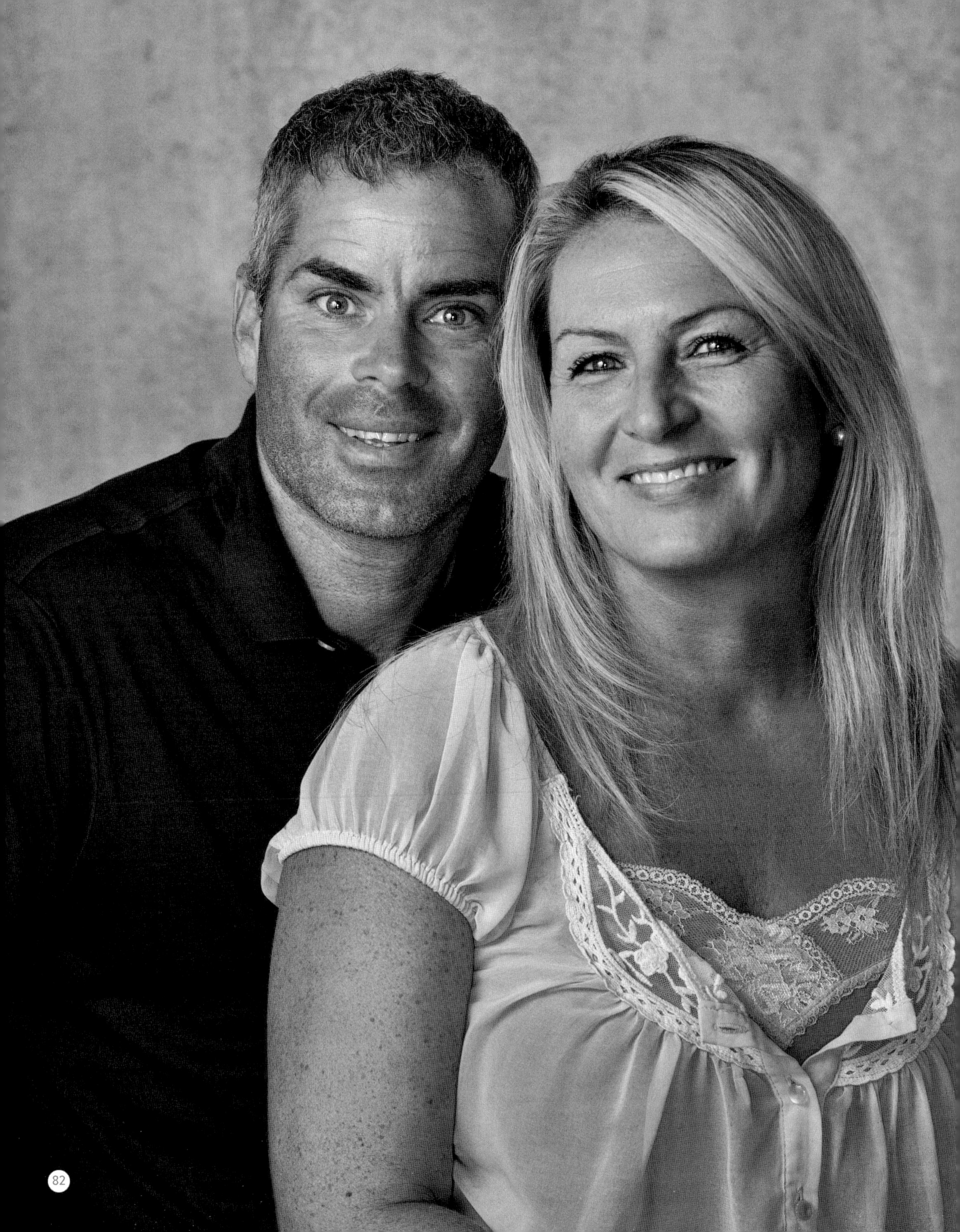

SAM & KAREN

Manchester and Corby

"At first the drugs had very little place in our lives. I thought I could change him. Unbeknownst to me he was very wounded and so was I," described Karen.

Sam, with his addictive personality, easily distracted Karen from the pain of going through a divorce by excessively caring for her. At first their relationship was casual fun, but their bond went much deeper as the years went by. As Sam's addiction to alcohol, crack and later heroin increased, their relationship was on and off for a period of time. Once he confessed the totality of the addictions, they tried traveling the world together as an attempt to break them. But the addictions followed even in paradise.

There were periods of time when Sam would temporarily replace his drug addiction with other things like golf. During these times Karen would come back into his life only to leave again when the drugs returned. Ever since Sam was young he said he felt like he was never good enough. These feelings continued as an adult and he told me, "Even though I was successful outwardly, inside I was in turmoil. Nothing ever satisfied. The drugs were the solution to switching that thinking off so I didn't care."

Sam tried everything to get out of the mess he was in: rehabs, counseling, even a stay at a Greek monastery. "I could have written a thesis about addiction. I studied it, I also lived it, and I knew addiction. But I couldn't have told you one thing about the solution. I had no idea I had a spiritual problem."

Sam finally found the kind of help that really worked when he came to Betel. He had an encounter: a meeting with Jesus that moved him. He felt instantly freed. His detox was mild even though his body was full of all kinds of substances. He regained his physical strength and health in record time. But he hadn't had a deep transformational healing in his heart, the kind that changes one's inner world. And he began to use again.

Although their intentions were good and they married, Sam and Karen soon went back to the only way they knew to live: hurting each other. The big difference this time was that Sam described his behavior as "a religious nut case". He had experienced some freedom and deliverance but he had not experienced the fullness that God intended.

Now recognizing their need for help, they both entered Betel and began a journey of humbly seeking God. They started their relationship anew, learning how to argue without destroying each other and how to be married with God in the center.

Sam went from being an absolutely hedonistic, pleasure-seeking man, to strict, judgmental and critical, and finally to a man who really loved people and had compassion for other's needs. God softened him, changed his inner world, healed his marriage and even blessed him with a son. The energy, generosity and hospitality of this couple is astounding.

Sam and Karen say about their lives now, "If it was just God, Jesus and our calling to Betel, it would have been enough. We were so grateful with being delivered into such a destiny and such a hope. And God has continued to add to us, giving us a son and many spiritual children. God just keeps on adding to us.

STEPHEN

Wigan

Stephen was a single parent until his son was seven when Stephen entered into a long-term relationship. Unfortunately, during the next seven years Stephen immersed himself in heroin and ended up in prison. Once out of prison, with his relationship over, it was decided that his son would come to live with him. It looked like a new house and a new drug-free life was in his future but only three months later it came crashing down again.

"Three months after promising my 14-year-old son I'd be there for him, I was sticking needles in my arms again. My son was devastated. My guilt and shame were too much to bear and I decided to end my tormented life. During the last few moments of my suicide attempt I cried out to God asking Him to understand why I was ending my life and hoping there would be some kind of forgiveness. I felt Jesus speaking to me without words. I got up and walked to a nearby church; it was Sunday. There I gave what was left of my life to Jesus."

Stephen had come to terms with the fact that his family and children wanted nothing to do with him anymore because of the pain he had caused over the years. But God had other plans.

Through the next eight years in Betel, as he walked his journey of healing, all of those relationships were restored to better than ever before. He is thankful that the relationships with his son and his other children are now healthy and full.

"My guilt and shame were too much to bear and I decided to end my tormented life."

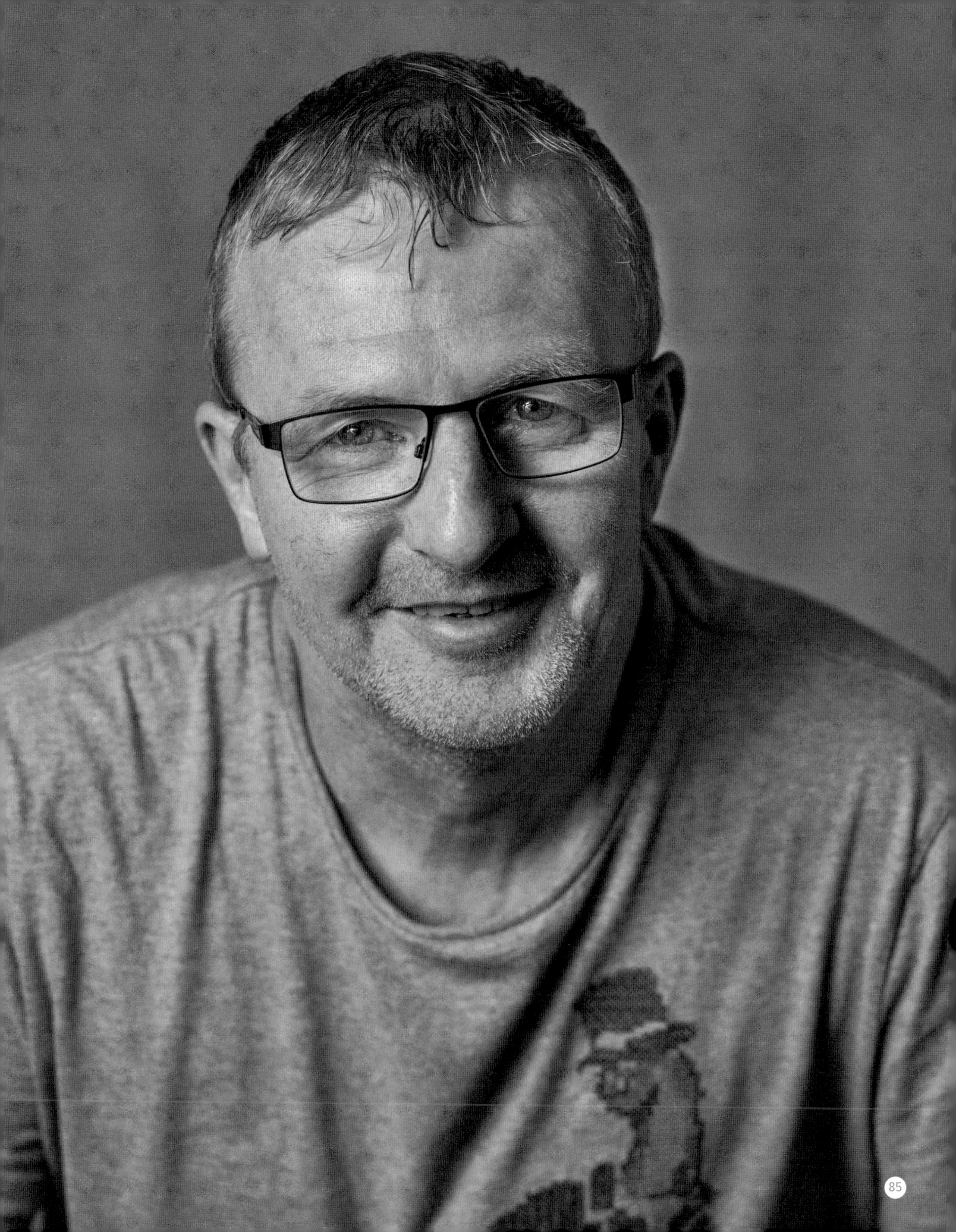

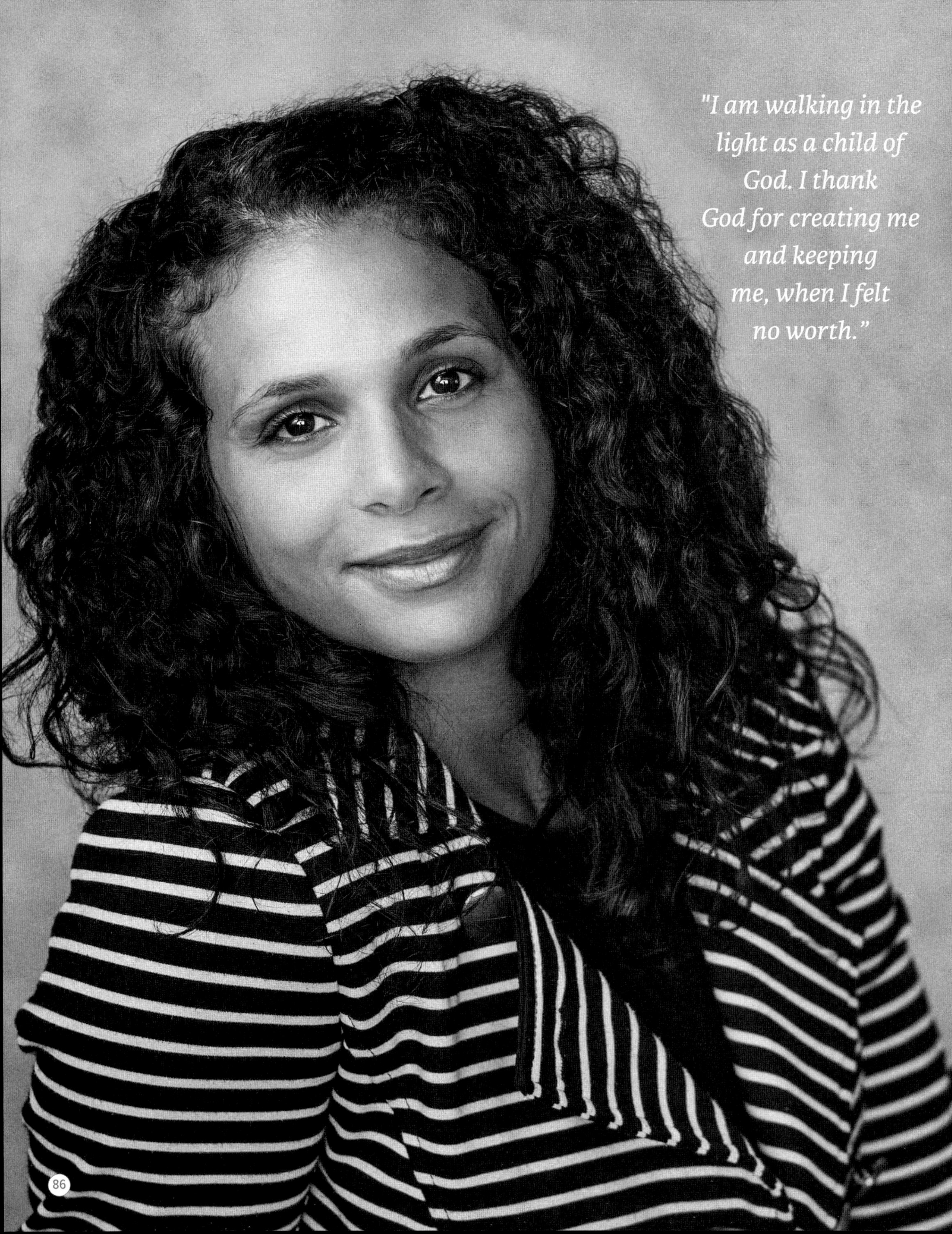

"I am walking in the light as a child of God. I thank God for creating me and keeping me, when I felt no worth."

KELLY

London

"I was a mess. I had no one to turn to for help. I was wild, so I began a cycle of running away, new man, new baby, drugs, alcohol, and violence. Repeat."

Kelly grew up with a mother who struggled with alcoholism and experienced a lot of violence from the men in her life. Unfortunately, Kelly and her younger brother were exposed to it as well. At seven or eight, Kelly and her brother watched in horror as a boyfriend beat their mom into someone unrecognizable—because she had refused to cuddle Kelly on the bus. At ten years old, Kelly again witnessed the rape and beating of her mom by this man. The next morning Kelly called a crisis hotline and they were taken to a safe house and never saw that man again.

Things went from bad to worse as Kelly and her brother became victims of violence themselves. They were taken to a children's home where Kelly was sexually abused by a 14-year-old girl. "I was crying out for comfort, love and attention, but this attention confused me. I was terrified and full of fear. I wet the bed till I was 12 and I couldn't sleep in the dark."

At age 15, Kelly had started taking cocaine and by 16 she was taking all types of drugs, pills, speed, and smoking heroin. Since both of her biological parents were addicts it was easy to score and use at any time. At 17 she had her first of five children. "I felt so empty and numb. I just wanted to feel loved, wanted and normal."

Life became even more unbearable the day her brother, who was everything to her, went missing. "I lost control, I wanted to die. I would lay in my bed hoping to die in my sleep. I would get so wrecked, I didn't care about anything."

Years later a woman named Nadya from a local church came to their house and brought three bags of groceries. Over the next two years, Kelly saw her steady lovingkindness and pondered if there was more to life than the way she had been living. "I didn't want to live this selfish, cold, dirty lifestyle anymore—I wanted change."

It was through the patient help and prayers of Nadya that Kelly found the help she desperately needed in the form of Betel. Walking through the doors she had a sense of belonging she couldn't understand, but she felt peace. "The biggest battle I faced was forgiveness for all that had happened. God was by my side and we faced it together. In God's perfect timing I overcame my past. He delivered me and I began to forgive everyone who hurt me and ultimately, myself."

Kelly says, "I am finally [at age 35] no longer afraid of the darkness. I am walking in the light as a child of God. I thank God for creating me and keeping me, when I felt no worth."

Kelly has a deep compassion for people who are living like she did, and to help moms and their children find hope. She wants to be a light in the darkness and to say, "You don't have to live like that anymore."

ANDY

South Wales

"I was spiraling slowly out of control for years. I was selling and using drugs but it wasn't until I started heroin that I lost everything."

Andy grew up in a deprived town where a lot of drug use was the norm, and joblessness common. He began taking drugs at 15 and started selling almost right away. This continued for ten years.

"I lived in a small room with just a bed in the worst part of my town. I went to a drop-in center[1] to basically get food and have something to do with my time." Here is where he met someone who was similar to him but had found a way out of the addiction. He kept a watchful eye on this guy and saw that he experienced a real lasting change. This other man's story kept him coming back to hear more and it gave Andy hope for his own life.

Once Andy was introduced to Jesus he said that he grabbed Christ with both hands. Andy could see that it was real in his friend and he was desperate for change in his own life. "I felt a joy like I hadn't experienced for years and years since I was a kid, that sort of feeling. That is what drew me."

Now nine years in Betel, Andy has chosen to serve as a leader in Betel's Hexham work in Northeast England, helping to run a large gardening business as he models freedom and wholeness to the center's forty men.

[1]A drop-in center is a service agency for either the mentally ill, homeless, teenagers, and others, offering a place where people can go to obtain food and other services.

"I felt a joy like I hadn't experienced for years and years since I was a kid, that sort of feeling. That is what drew me."

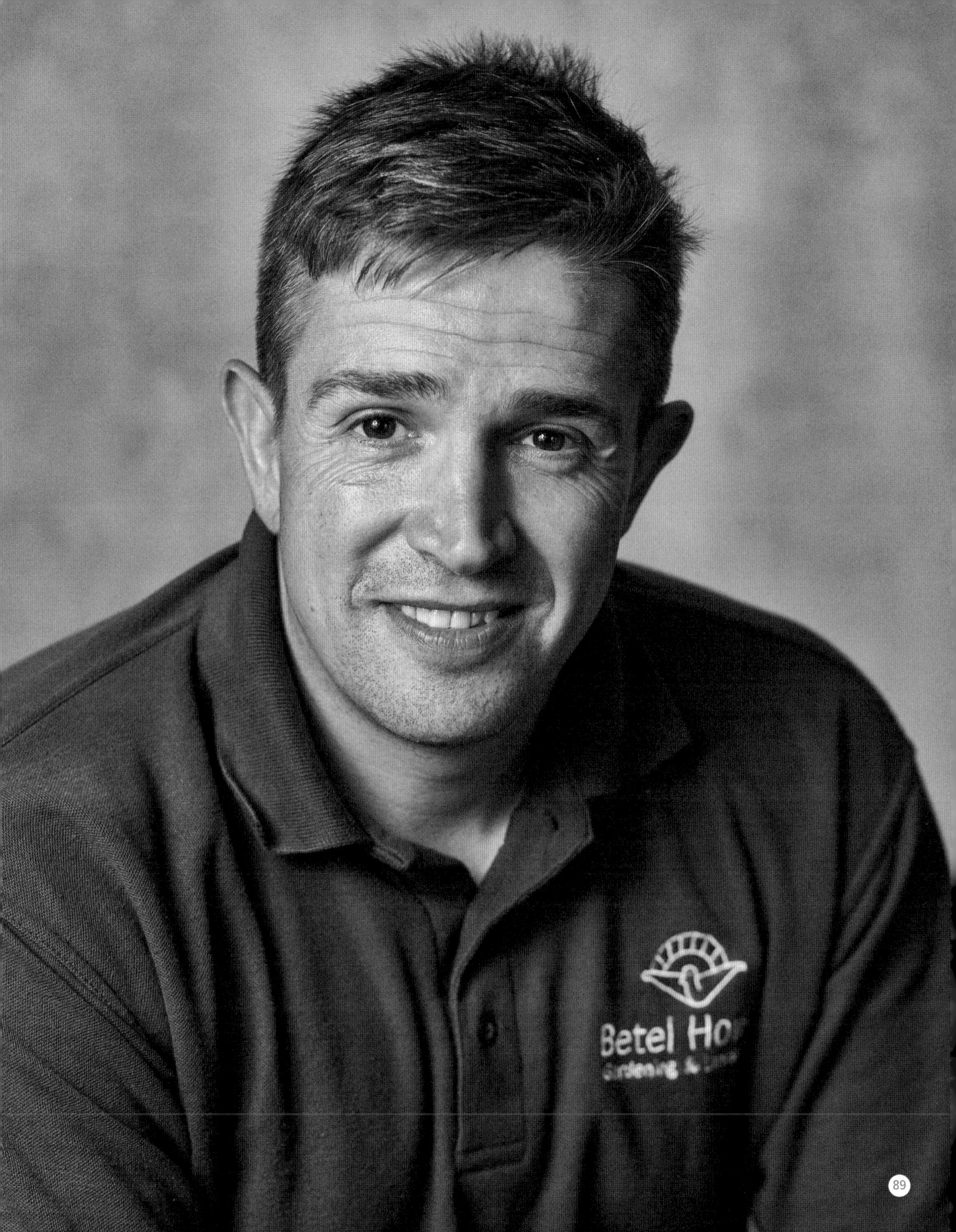
Betel

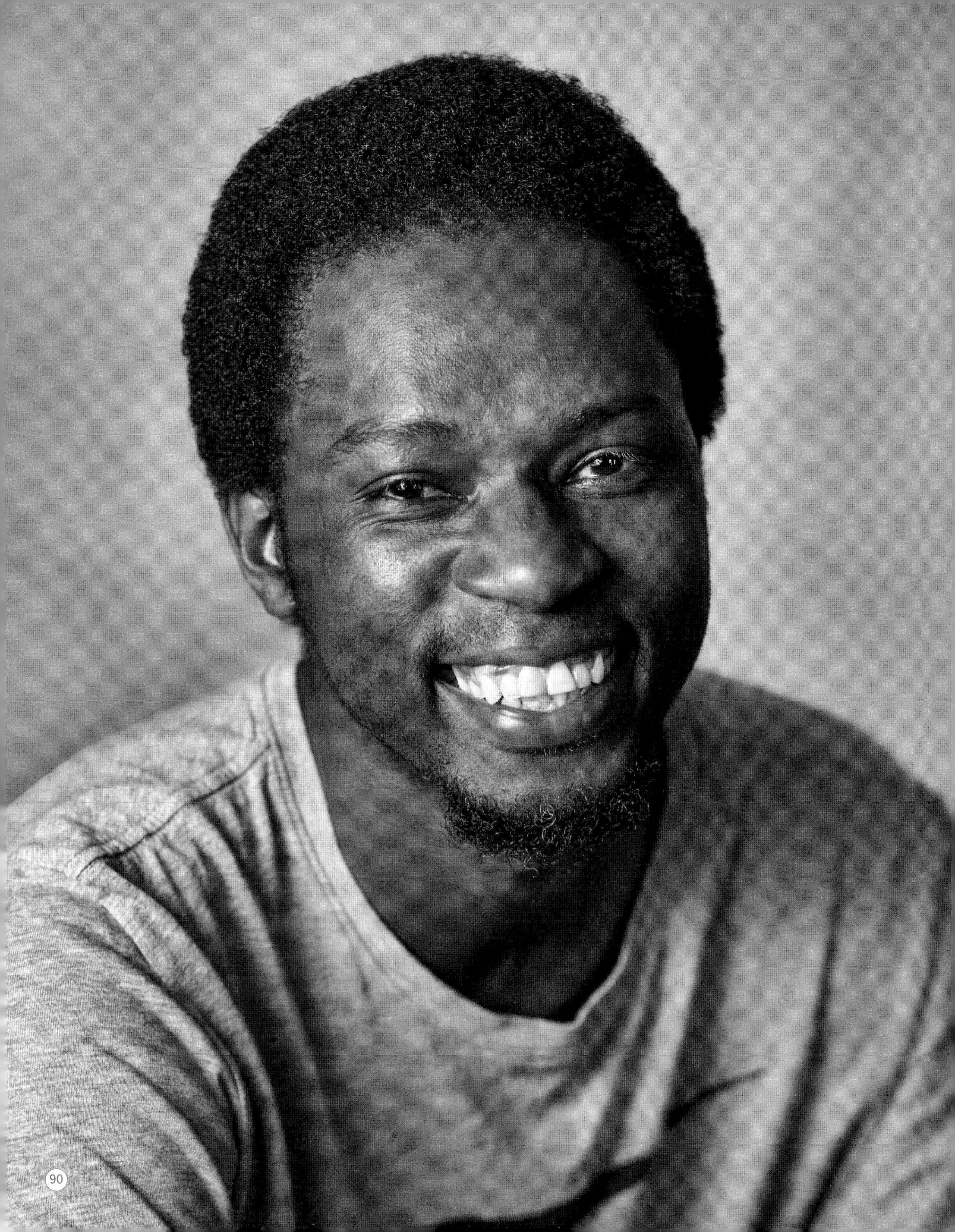

SEKOU

Zambia

"The only memories I remember of my family were when I was bleeding after being beaten by my father, or of my mother being beaten."

Sekou felt abandoned because he believed that no one could help him. Rejection and loneliness were the result of ten years of family trauma. At age 12, Sekou ran away to his uncle's home. This is where he began drinking to battle the worries of life. Sekou shared, "It gave me confidence, a sense of acceptance and made me feel like I was loved by the people I drank with."

He thought alcohol didn't hurt him. "It's legal, I can buy it whenever I want and it's there for me all the time," he reasoned. For many years he was in and out of hospitals because of alcohol-related issues, but he still rejected the idea of having any alcohol problems. It wasn't until he woke up in a hotel room, in a pool of blood with someone screaming, that he began to come to his senses. After being taken to the hospital that night, he ran away, searching for something to drink. That experience helped him realize he needed help with his alcoholism.

Sekou's search for answers ultimately brought him to the community of Betel. After being at Betel for three days, he was once again taken to a hospital. This time the doctors couldn't even help him. They wanted to section him (hold him for mental health reasons). But God had other plans for him: plans to help him heal.

Sekou now says, "I've gone from a person that no one could help to a man that God uses to help others. All I wanted was a good life but I didn't know which way to take, I didn't know the truth about myself."

The peace and confidence that poured out of Sekou when he sat across from me was proof of a changed life. His quick smile and soft-spoken way were relationally comfortable. The evident change in Sekou has made a way for healing and restoration with his father. They have reached a healing point in which they both were able to confess, for the first time, that they love each other.

Sekou says, "All my life I believed I would never amount to anything. I thought I would always be a failure and that fear would always have a grip on me. But Jesus delivered me from my fears. He turned my fear into faith. I want to follow Him for the rest of my life."

"I've gone from a person that no one could help to a man that God uses to help others."

DAVE

Nottingham

"I committed crime nearly every day, I stole, lied, and cheated. I lost everything and everyone close to me. I tried countless times to get off drugs and failed."

At 13, Dave started smoking cannabis which quickly led to smoking heroin. Dave graduated school with a diploma and addictions to crack and heroin. "I accepted in my heart that the best I'll ever be is an addict. That place is a desperate, lonely place where to die seems the only way out."

Years later, Dave ran into an old friend who was now clean and heard him talk about Jesus. Dave thought his friend was crazy. This friend used to have the same life Dave had but now he was so different. He was confident, he was leading worship, preaching, directing a Betel center, had a wife and a beautiful little girl. Dave thought, "That's what I want. It's always what I wanted." Those dreams had slipped away a long time ago. But seeing his friend—who had been just like him and now had his life together—gave him hope.

After learning that his friend's dramatic change really did hinge on Jesus, he thought "I really have nothing to lose in trying Jesus." After he choose to follow Jesus for himself, he began to see things in a completely new way. "It really felt like I was living life blind. I didn't see life for what it was. I only could see my very small portion. I started to see a whole lot of things. I began to be annoyed with myself for letting myself walk around in that darkness, not ever aware that there was darkness! It was just normal for me."

Dave noted that so often we can be in darkness but we can't see it; we don't even know we are in the dark. There is no choice of light or dark until something shifts our perspective. Now that Dave sees so clearly, his perspective is full of hope. "God delivers so much more, so much bigger and better. Every year God seems to do something amazing. In the last five years I've been excited when I look to a new year, thinking, 'What is God going to do this year?!' "

"I accepted in my heart that the best I'll ever be is an addict."

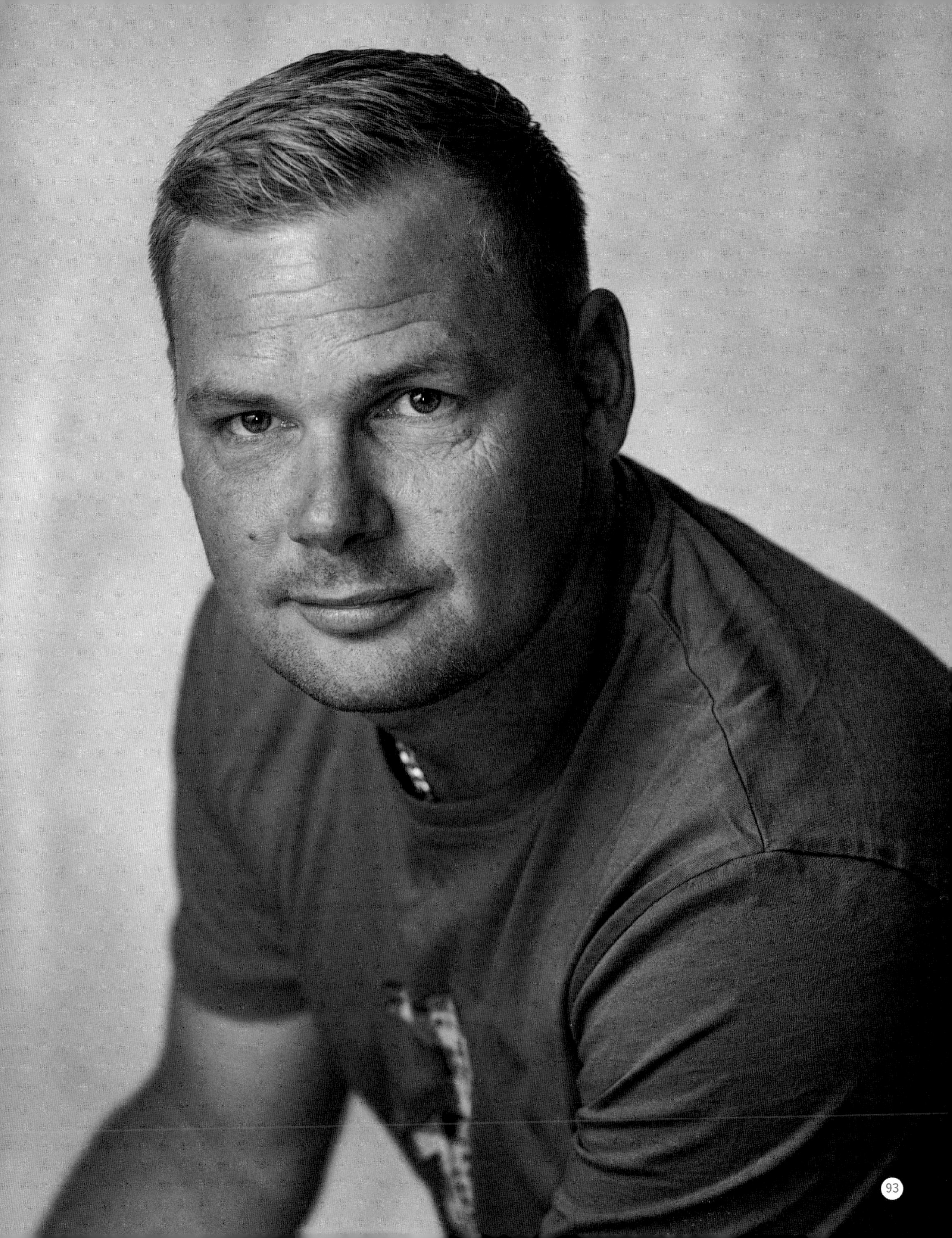

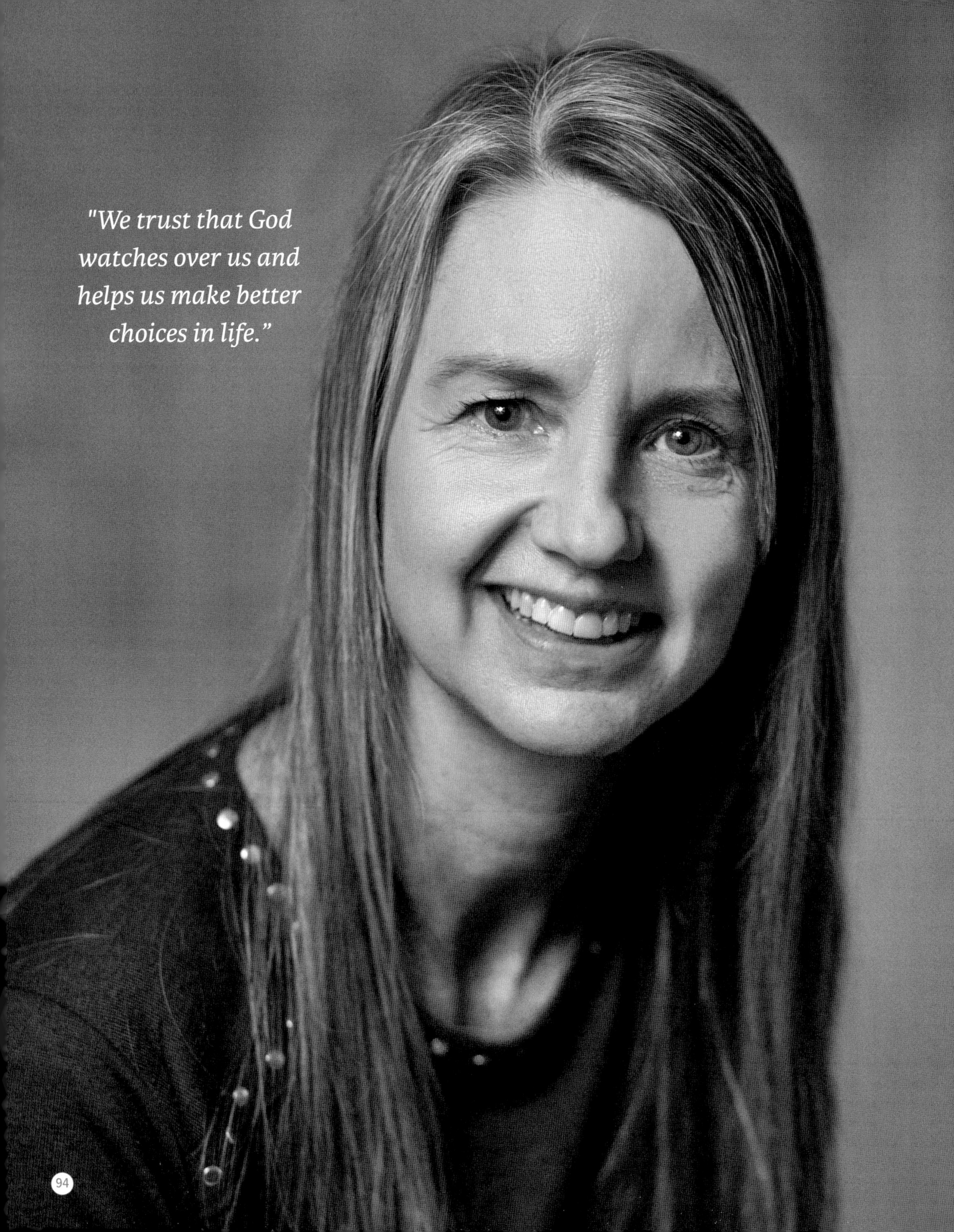
"We trust that God
watches over us and
helps us make better
choices in life."

DEENA

South Africa

Deena grew up in South Africa with a dysfunctional mother. After being badly abused physically and mentally for 14 years, her alcoholic mother finally left the family. Her father joined the Jehovah's Witnesses and forced the kids to do the same. Deena hated the Jehovah's Witness church and felt like it contributed to the abuse she received from other children at school. Deena told me, "Growing up, I always felt like there was something wrong with me, that I was 'weird' for my mother not to love me."

In her 20s, Deena left her father's faith and hit the party scene taking recreational drugs and drinking. This led to her father disowning her. After being in a car-jacking, Deena was jarred into the reality of how short life was. The desire to travel came out of this experience and within the year she was on her way to Britain. In the UK she no longer took drugs but she entered into what she called, "working hard and playing hard." Alcohol was her way of fitting in and being accepted.

She got married and after finding out children weren't possible, their marriage deteriorated and ended in divorce. She said that "a part of me always wanted to have children and especially my own little girl to whom I could 'give back' what I lacked from my own mother. There was an emptiness in me that needed filling. Even though my mother was gone, I always longed for a 'mother's love'." As a result of this great loss, Deena continued to drink to ease the pain.

Another relationship began but became mentally abusive. Deena became pregnant only to be convinced to abort the baby. After the abortion she told me, "I hated myself for it. My life went downhill from there." She returned to alcohol and spiraled downwards. She eventually lost her job, her driver's license, and even her home. While living on the streets, she was physically beaten so badly she ended up in the hospital. She begged the hospital staff to help her but they could only offer another detox which had failed to help her in the past. She felt completely hopeless. Thankfully a couple of weeks later she stumbled upon a leaflet for Betel which said, "We can take you almost the next day."

"Betel has not been easy, but if it was not for Betel, I would not have a relationship with Jesus and freedom from drugs and alcohol," Deena said. After a time of healing she met Lenny who was also at Betel. Now they are married and she says, "Life is so different for Lenny and me today. I work in the administration office for Betel in Scotland and we trust that God watches over us and helps us make better choices in life."

As I sat and talked with Deena, it was difficult to imagine her in the broken state she described. Her restoration is so complete.

RASOOL

Bermuda

It was a cold, winter day in New York City when Rasool, out of money with no place to go, sat on a bench across from a Chinese restaurant. He cried out silently, "Oh God, I'm so hungry!" A man came out of the Chinese place and sat down behind him. Rasool again breathed a prayer, "God please don't let him eat all his food." The man took four bites and threw the box in the trash. Rasool had never eaten from the trash before. But tears stung his eyes as he reached for the hot, barely touched food, believing that God had heard his prayer.

In Rasool's childhood, there wasn't much, if any, stability. His home and family were shattered by physical abuse from his father. One foster home after another left Rasool struggling to understand his own identity. The effects of all his experiences left him splintered.

However, at the age of 13, Rasool had an encounter with the love of Jesus that marked him for life. He felt the love of Jesus deeply. The only thing that never changed during this period was Jesus. Through the years he would feel the presence and love of God in unique and various ways.

Moving to New York City from Bermuda seemed like the thing to do at 17. He quickly found acceptance in the gay lifestyle. He said, "I love women but I just felt acceptance there." He lived as a woman for one year going so far as moving towards a sex change. He and his friends would prostitute themselves to fuel their crack addiction. During this time he experienced amazing miracles but he couldn't bring himself to give his life to God. It caused a lot of turmoil. Contemplating suicide at one point, he thought "There has got to be a way out of this. I don't even know who I am."

At one point, Rasool remembers saying to God, "I don't want to serve you because it's a waste of time; I've tried too many times, only to let you down again." He went on to say, "I just didn't understand why God kept pursuing me." If he returned to his own self-serving ways, he was uncomfortable. But when he tried to follow Christ he felt like a failure. There was no peace for him anywhere. He did not feel comfortable being labeled either "gay" or "straight." He was whatever he felt like at the moment. He saw no way out of his cycles.

People would try to help him, but they simply didn't know what to do with a man who sought to pursue God in his life yet would turn around and prostitute himself high on crack. It wasn't until later that Rasool found out that not everyone had given up on him like he thought. He discovered that the one woman he met at 13 when he first asked Jesus into his life, had prayed for him every day for 12 years.

Today, after giving into God's relentless pursuit, Rasool is a confident man who walks in freedom from confusion. Rasool spent a number of years at Betel, gradually growing in responsibility to become a house leader and working as a chef at Betel's busy Rising Cafe in Coventry. He recently married and is now pursuing full time ministry in Wales.

God stuck with Rasool when no one else did. Now, the presence of God overwhelms him all the time and he says, "God's love never gets old!"

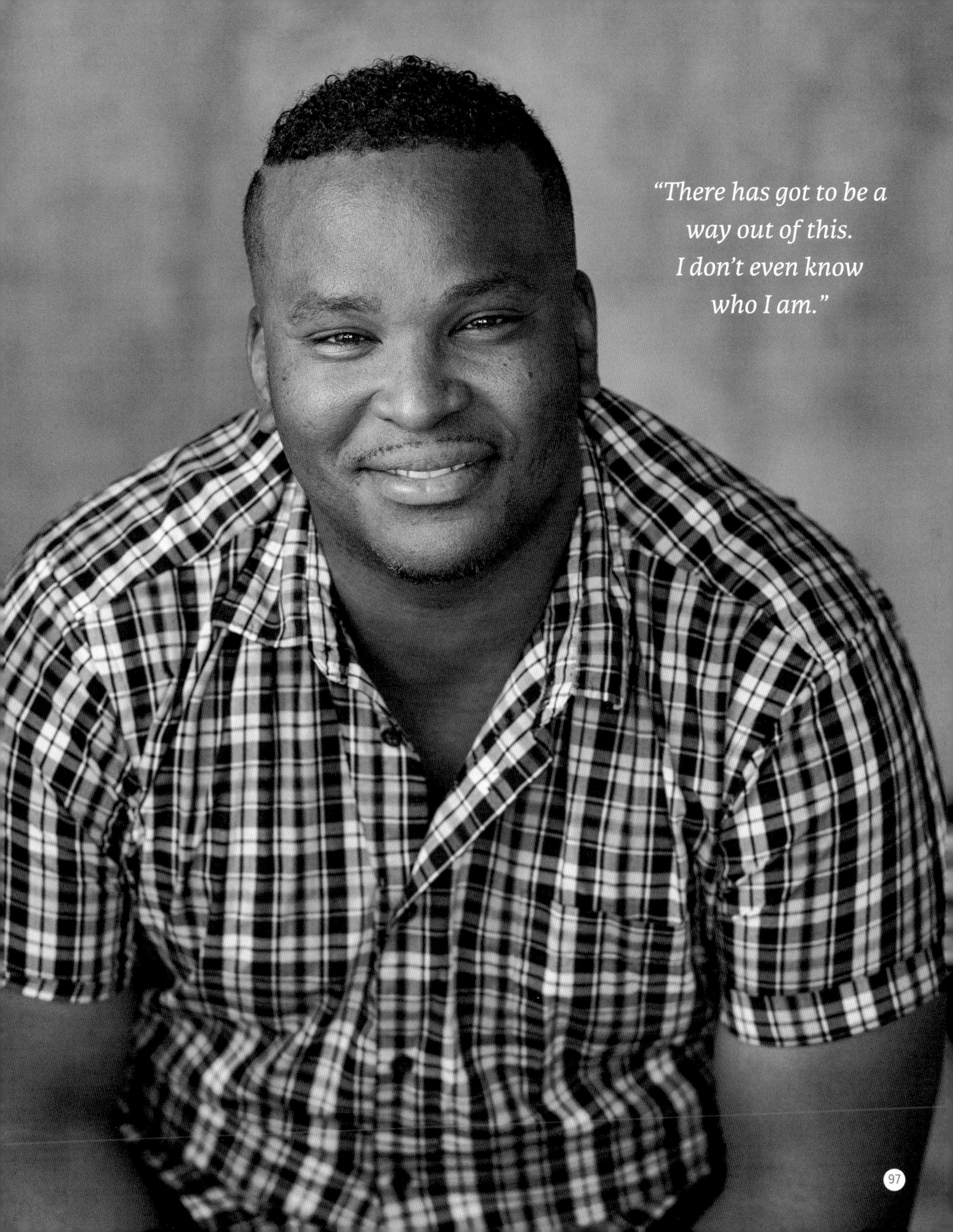

"There has got to be a way out of this. I don't even know who I am."

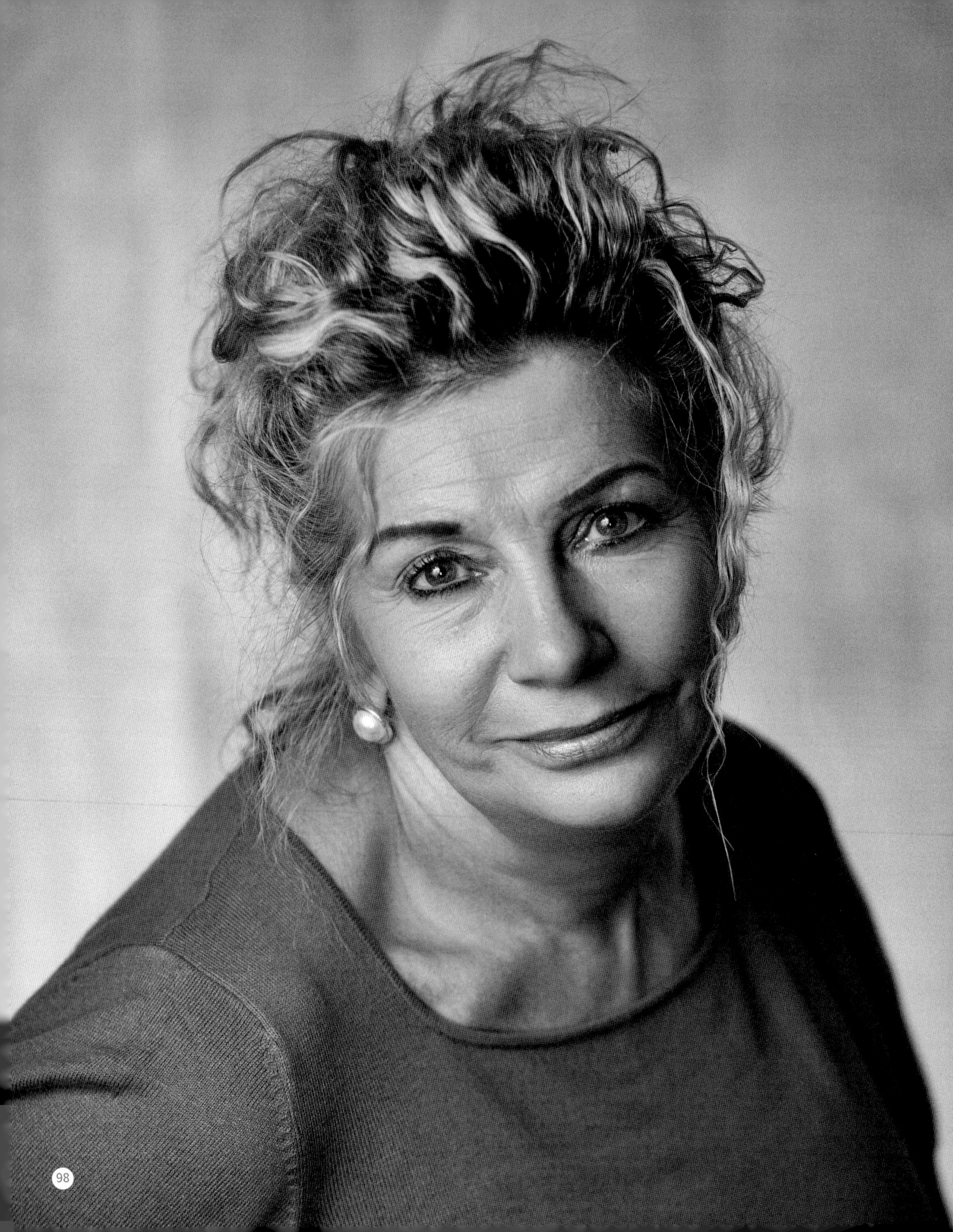

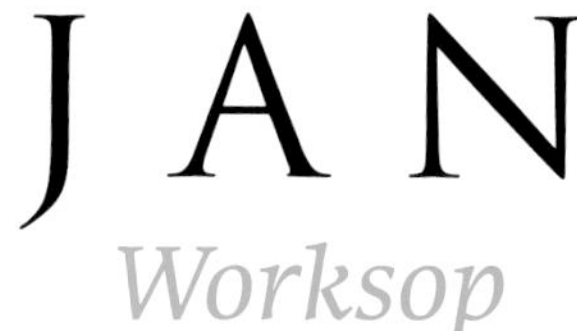

Worksop

"It can happen to you very quickly and easily. It can happen to any of us irrespective of education or social status. It's arrogant to think we are above it."

Sometimes assumptions are made as to what kind of person becomes an addict. Jan was one of those people that you would never have expected to be one.

At age 42, Jan's life suddenly changed. Just before Christmas she received a phone call from a woman, claiming that she was having an affair with her husband. Jan was completely blindsided.

Shortly after receiving this news, Jan was diagnosed with Crohn's disease which rendered her incapable of normal day-to-day functioning. So much so, she had to leave her job. She struggled to even care for herself due to the severity of the illness. Eventually losing the use of her legs she became wheelchair bound. Her children left to live with their dad and she even lost her home. As a result she began drinking more and more to numb the pain.

Out of heartache and loneliness she started a relationship with a colleague at the hospital where she had worked. After a time it became terribly abusive. "He tied me up with ropes and broke my bones. He tried to drown me. I remember him bringing me up [out of the water] and all I could do was cough and sputter." He always got out of trouble with the law because he would lie and blame things on Jan's excessive drinking. It was Jan's sister who encouraged her to break away before it was too late.

In this state of brokenness, the community of Betel embraced Jan and patiently introduced her to hope. "Jesus gave me freedom from my addiction. He renewed and transformed my life. Where once only darkness and despair lived, now lives love, joy and adventure. It has been a difficult yet exciting time finding out who I am, being accepted for myself. I've invited Jesus into my life and allowed Him to heal those deep and painful wounds. I've regained my self-worth and confidently know my purpose in life. I'm now able to move forward with a peace and a joy, knowing that I am ready for whatever life brings my way."

Jan is now whole from head to toe, the wheelchair long gone. For many years she has been leading and helping hundreds of other women find spiritual and physical healing from addiction.

"Where once only darkness and despair lived, now lives love, joy and adventure."

TIMON

Manchester

"I had real destructive rage at one point in my life. It was the sort of rage that I turned inward on myself. I lived my whole life basically destroying my life in different areas. I was consumed by rage and anger."

The absence of his father had a devastating impact on Timon. The rejection, anger, and self-destructive behavior started early and went on for 27 years. Filling the hole in his life with drugs only made the hole bigger and deeper. Injecting heroin daily led him to spending £800 (or over $1000) a day.

Timon had many run-ins with Jesus through the years, even asking Him into his life at one point. Yet, he struggled with addiction continually. He says it was all about surrender for him. "I resisted the call to surrender my life to Christ. I wanted all the benefits of the Christian life but was unwilling to really lay my life down." It came down to his inability to trust that God was actually good. He wondered how he could trust this God with his life.

"Many times I cried out to God from the depths of my addiction, found help, and recovery, only to try and take control of my own life again. This cycle continued for 15 years and always ended up with me becoming a slave again to my addiction." Once, while in a rehab, he went to a revival meeting in Scotland. He responded to the altar call and found himself on the ground, unable to stand. He said, "It was like God was washing the anger out of me. When I stood up it was like God removed the destructive rage that controlled my life. Balance was restored. Through that I realized that God did something in me that I wouldn't be able to do in myself. It took a miracle to rid me of that."

The struggle to follow God or drugs was finally broken once Timon made a promise to God that he would really trust Him with his life. Weighing only 7 ½ stone (105 pounds) and close to death, Timon found a place that he could call home and healing began in earnest. "I recommitted my life to God and He met me in a way that totally changed how I saw myself, other people and ultimately God himself through Jesus. My life took on new meaning and I received healing from some of the very deepest hurts in my life."

Talking to Timon today, it is evident that he is a very grateful and gentle man. It flows out of him naturally. God has filled his deep need for a father by putting men in his life who have shown him acceptance and kindness. He no longer feels the need to impress or perform. Timon, who knew nothing but addictions and crime, is now married. He leads men in their businesses and is Betel's public relations representative. When he talked of his wife, his face lit up with such love and joy it made me smile. The lasting change in Timon is so vivid.

"I still have to pinch myself when I consider where I was all those years ago. I spent so many years trying to get clean. When I consider all that God has done for me, I think God must really love me to take the trouble to do that for me."

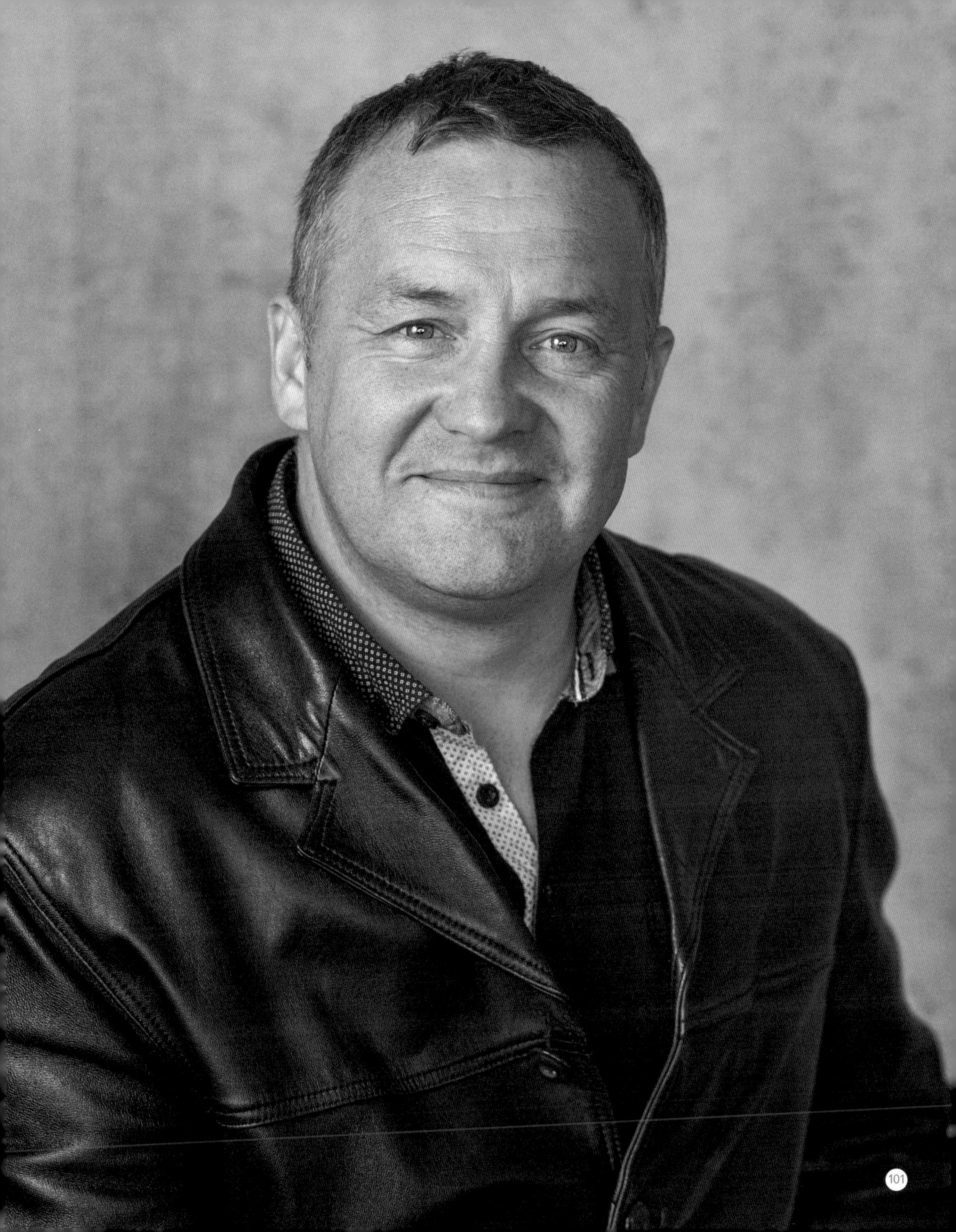

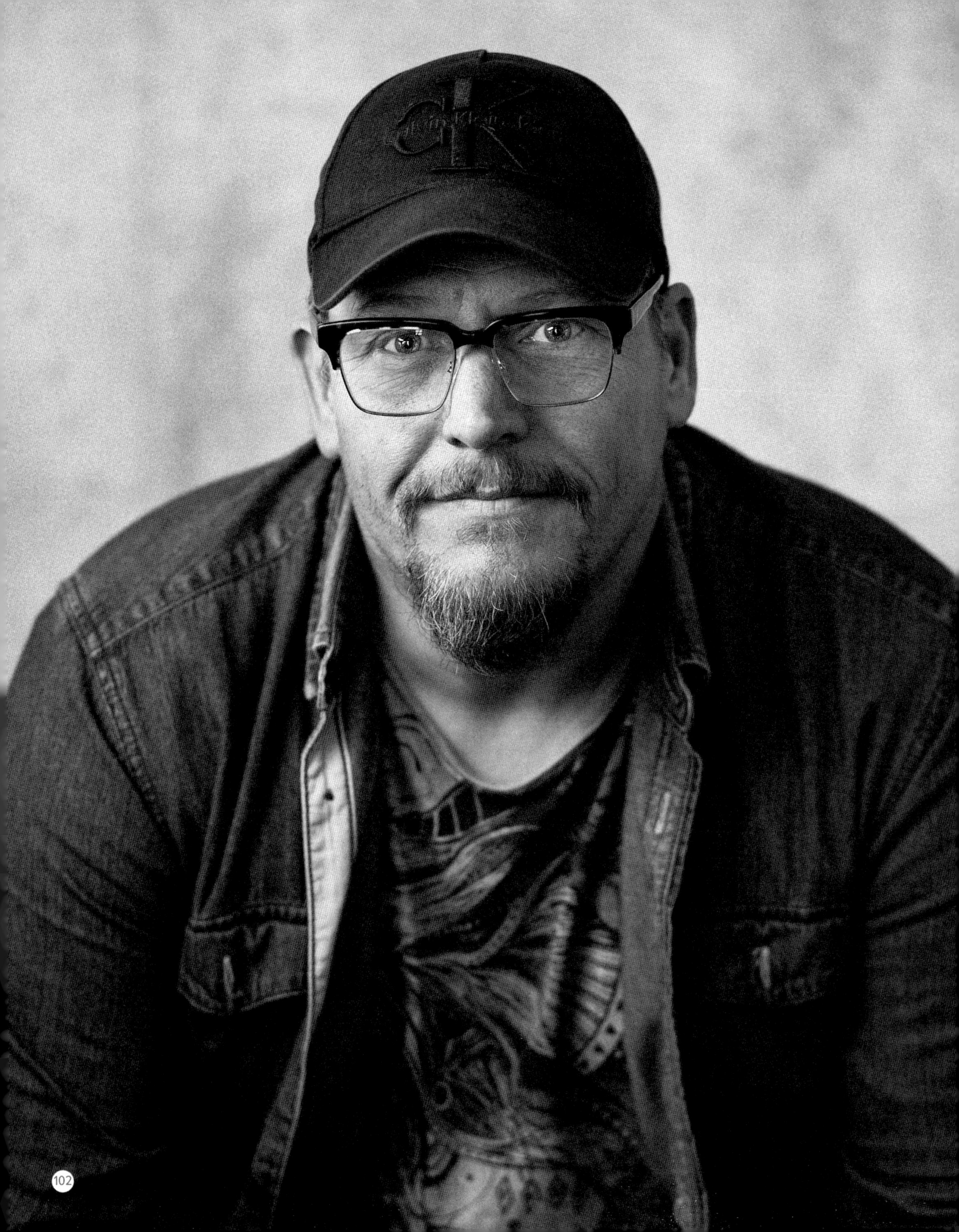

WAYNE

Leeds

Wayne grew up surrounded by crime in his family and his neighborhood. Cannabis, acid and speed were introduced to him at a very early age, which was normal for the people in his circles. Cocaine and heroin had him hooked right away at age 20. As his drug habit became more intense, the crimes he committed became more daring. "If something wasn't stuck down, we would take it," recalls Wayne. In and out of different prisons for crimes ranging from armed robbery to purse snatches to cutting open safes, led him to the point where he had no hope left.

"I actually thought there was no future for me. I finished a big jail sentence at 30 years of age. My reading and writing skills were very limited, I had few communication skills, and my people skills were next to zero. I was used to fighting for or taking what I wanted. So I thought my future was very bleak. I went to prison a junkie and came out one. I had no hope of ever changing and I remember my mum saying, 'If you don't change, you're gonna die.' "

Through various circumstances Wayne found himself at Betel. He thought the people there were quite crazy, but one night while going through the worst cold turkey withdrawal, he experienced God. He slept for the first time in two weeks! And this was just the beginning of his journey.

"God did something. Not only did I end up with a restored life, a hope and a future but I ended up with a wife. I thought I would just be another statistic on a sheet of paper, but God said no. God had and has a plan for me and my family so I just want to carry on seeing what He wants to do."

"Jesus took a hopeless, lifeless junkie and changed his story completely. I was dead in my life with no hope of ever changing and God changed it all," Wayne declares.

Wayne and his wife now help to lead Betel's Nottingham Center, sharing God's hope and love with other broken men and women.

"Jesus took a hopeless, lifeless junkie and changed his story completely. I was dead in my life with no hope of ever changing and God changed it all."

About Betel UK

Betel UK is an independent Christian charity for men, women and families affected by the hardships that lead to social exclusion, drug and alcohol abuse, long-term unemployment and ultimately homelessness.

Founded in 1996, Betel UK is a national success story. The organization is effective, sustainable and entirely independent, receiving no government funding. The charitable model is unique: it offers men, women and families opportunities to transform their lives through a peer-led, caring Christian community, plus engage in skilled work.

Many leave the community as entrepreneurs, mentors and even go on to run new Betel centers. In this way, Betel has grown internationally from its beginnings in Madrid, Spain, to helping desperate people in 100 cities and 25 nations around the globe.

Betel's centers are entirely free of charge and keep no waiting lists. All Betel asks of its residents is a sincere desire to change their life. If they're willing to work hard, attend daily worship, and become an active member of the community, then residents can turn their life around. This is the story of thousands that have found transformation in Betel and have gone on to help others like them.

Betel UK has welcomed many thousands of people into their community since opening its doors in 1996. Many of their residents say life at Betel feels like becoming a new member of an extended family. Betel is a safe, structured, family-like environment where there is consistent peer support. During the first few months each resident is assigned a brother- or sister-like mentor. As such, Betel is not a rehabilitation center or a clinical program with doctors or counsellors, where patients receive a medicated detox, but instead a place that provides an alternative model of recovery which has made a radical difference in many lives that were formerly in chaos.

During their stay, residents are given increasing responsibility at home and work as they show willingness, dependability and a supportive attitude towards others. Over time, Betel residents learn to care for others, oversee household routines, lead work teams and run businesses.

The end goal of Betel is to help people not only escape addiction, but become productive and trustworthy men and women of character when they leave the community.

Betel UK is part of the larger work of Betel International, which began in 1985 and is based in Madrid, Spain. Betel (Spanish for Bethel) received its first destitute men and women off the streets of Madrid through the pioneering work of a team of Worldwide Evangelization for Christ (WEC) International missionaries. Since that time more than 200,000 homeless and socially disadvantaged have been helped throughout Spain, Portugal, Italy, Germany, France, Czech Republic, Belgium, Finland, Estonia, Bulgaria, Central Asia, Russia, Ukraine, Kazakhstan, Ireland, Mongolia, North Africa, Australia, Argentina, Brazil, Mexico, South Africa and the UK.

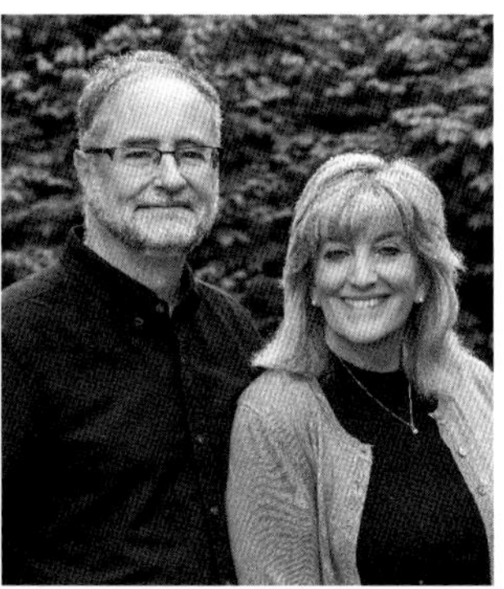

Kent and Mary Alice Martin are the directors of Betel UK.

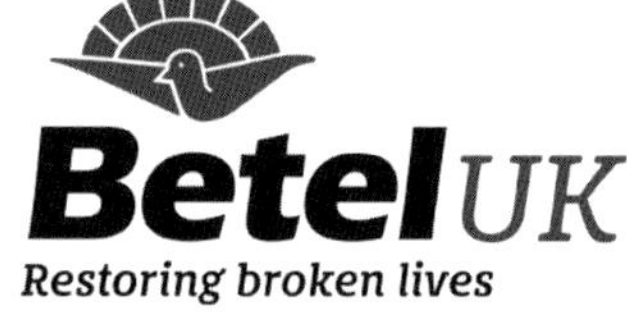

Acknowledgements

Thank you to Kent and Mary Alice Martin for having the faith in us to do this book project and for all the help and encouragement they have given throughout the process.

The Betel center directors were so hospitable during our visit to the UK and they made our time with them very comfortable. Thank you.

Each person featured in this book shared courageous and freely. I am so thankful for their selfless participation.

To our friends and family who continually encouraged us in this process I say thank you.

The group of church friends who prayed with us during our travels and during all the writing, I am grateful for the prayer coverage.

Thank you to Melodie Davis and Carolyn Stone for their editing and proofing expertise. With their help, I felt much more confident to just write and lean on them to help make sure it all made sense! Also thank you to others who helped with proofing along the way.

Lastly, thanks to Aaron, my husband, for believing in me and making the travel possible, as well as continually encouraging me to do the next step. I love you deeply.

—Christina Showalter

BIOGRAPHY

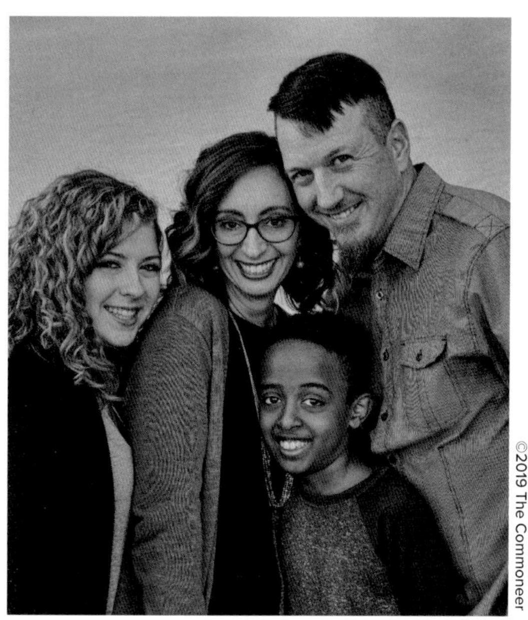

Christina Showalter has owned and operated a professional photography studio for 17 years. Her first book, *Escaping Addiction: Portraits of Hope and Restoration*, uniquely combines her passion for photography with her desire to share life-changing stories. She lives with her husband, Aaron, and two children, Elita and Sam in Harrisonburg, Virginia. As a family, they enjoy traveling together and dreaming big dreams. Grace Covenant Church is their home church.

THEN & NOW

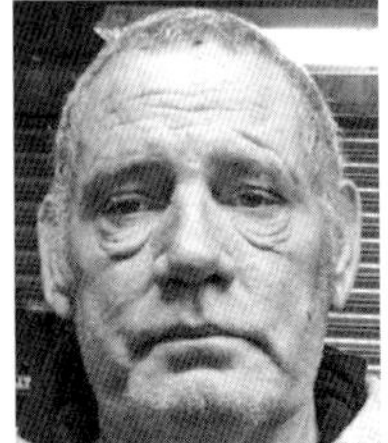

Adrian
pp. 48-49

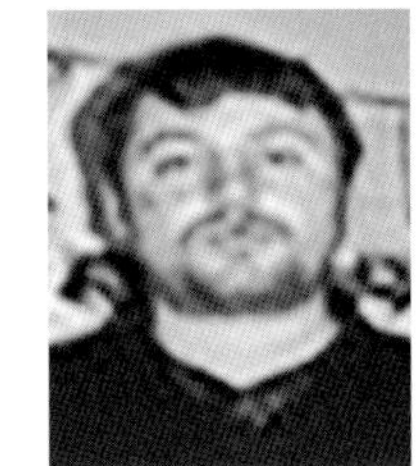

Alex
pp. 38-39

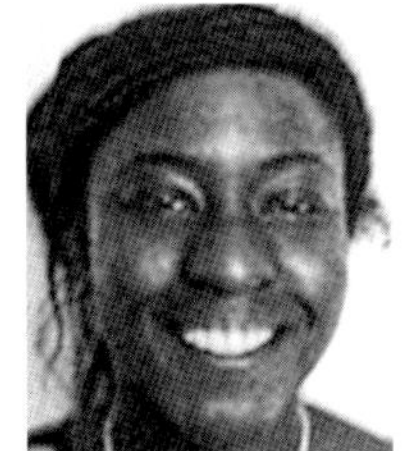

Allison
pp. 36-37

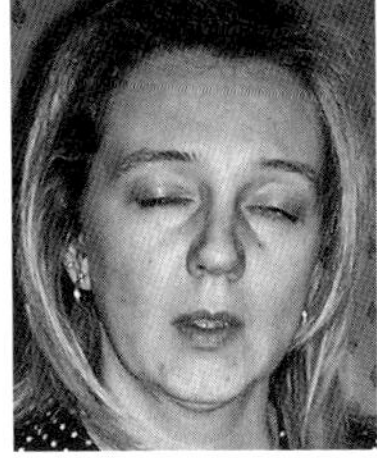
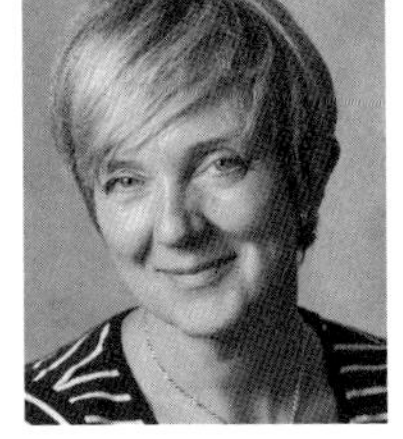

Amanda
pp. 14-15

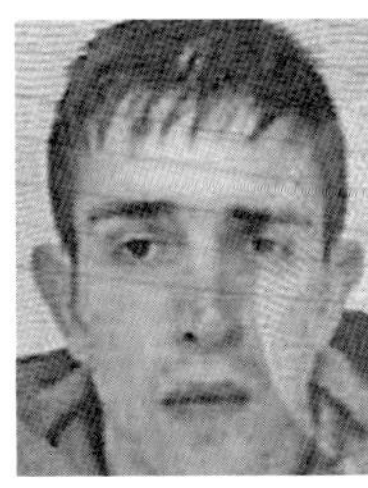

Andy
pp. 88-89

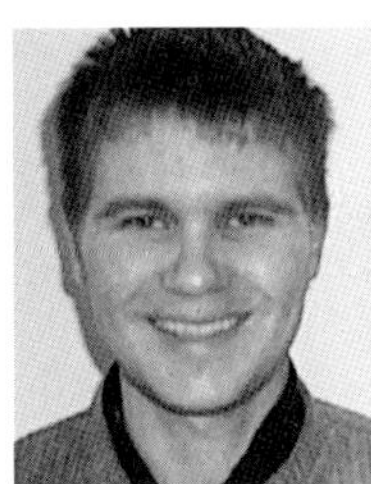

Anthony
pp. 54-55

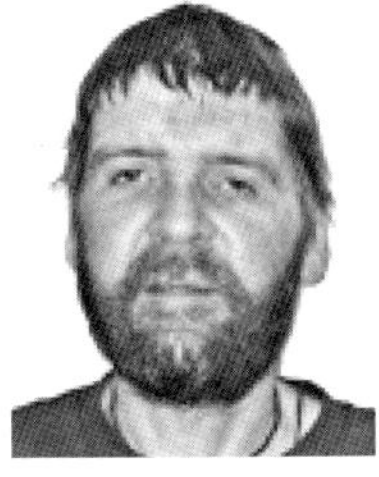
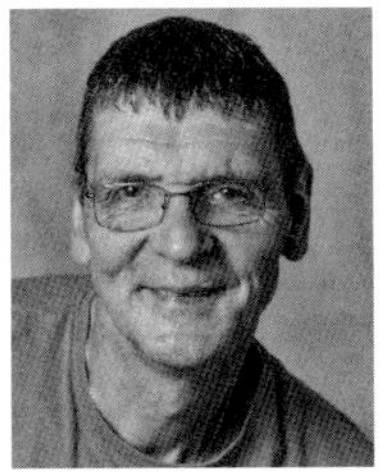
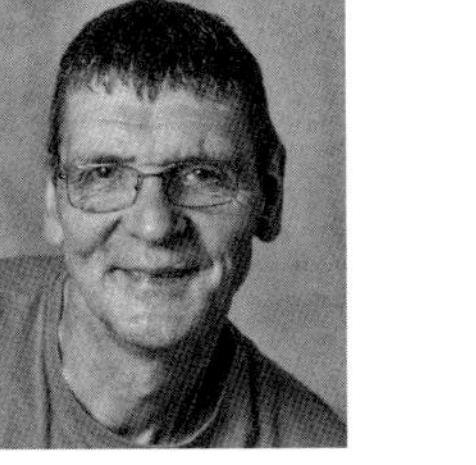

Austin
pp. 76-77

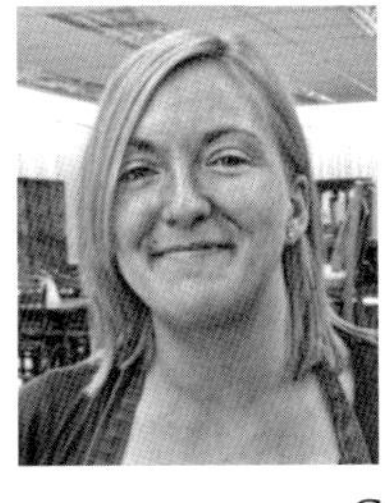
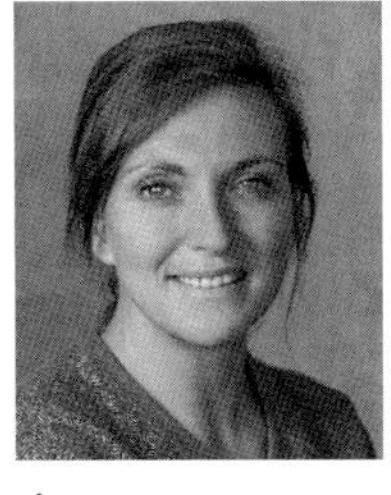

Ceri
pp. 50-51

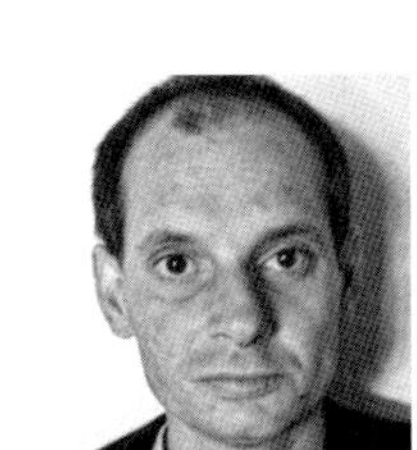
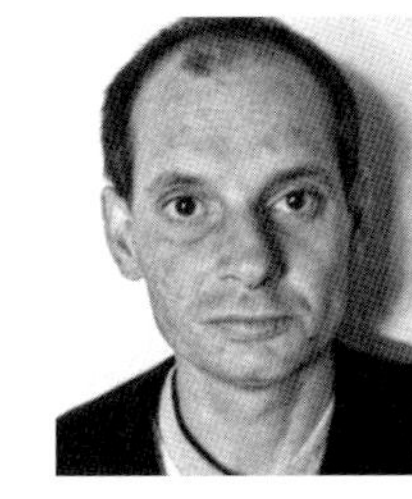
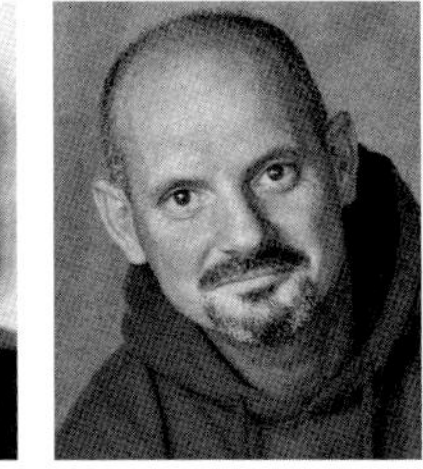

Craig
pp. 34-35

Dave
pp. 46-47

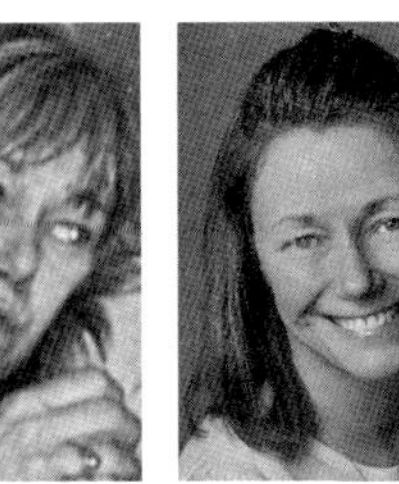
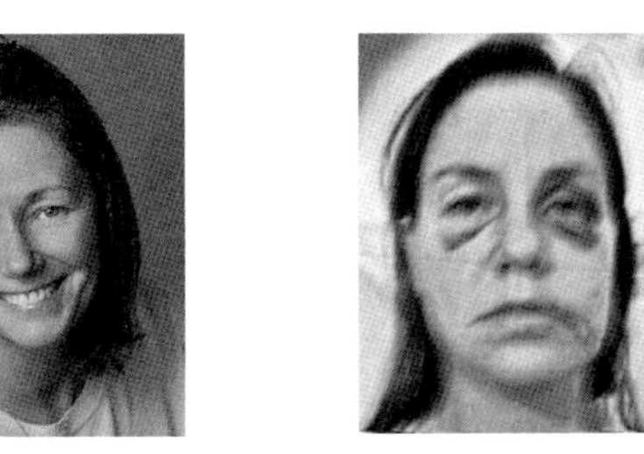

Dawn
pp. 60-61

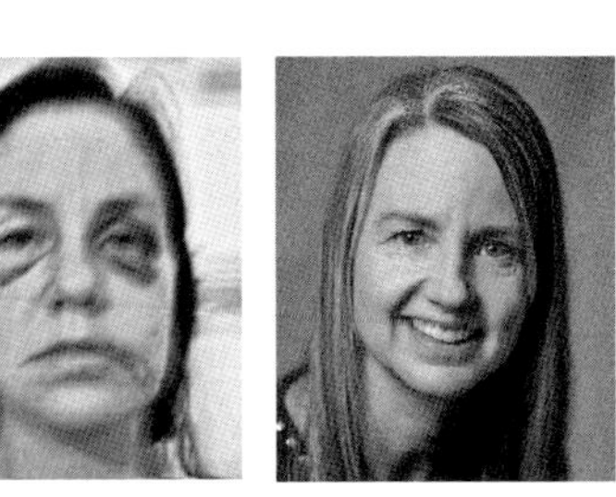

Deena
pp. 94-95

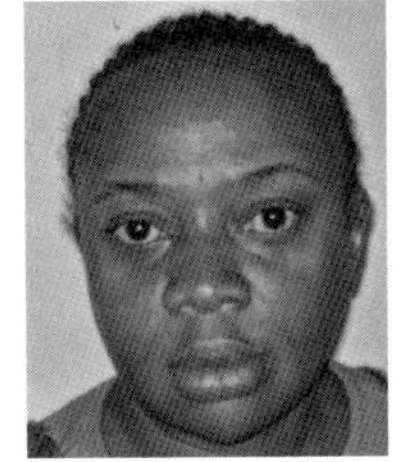
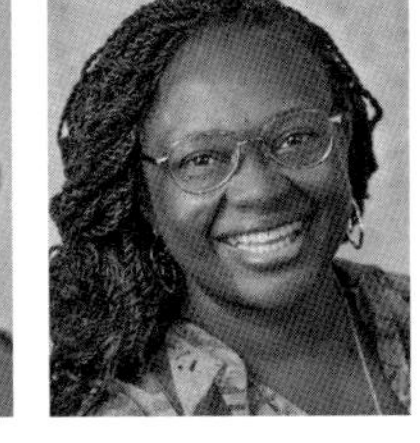
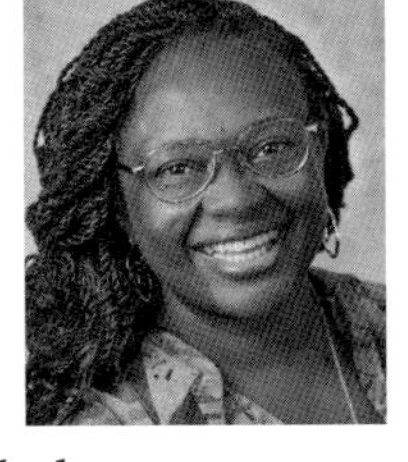

Ethel
pp. 18-19

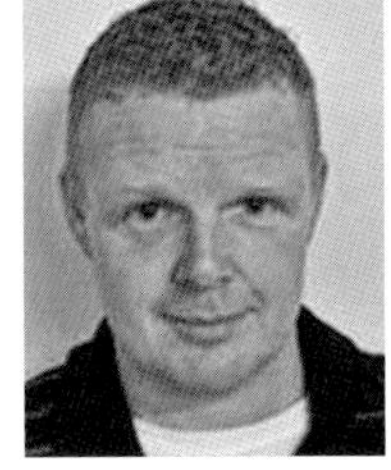
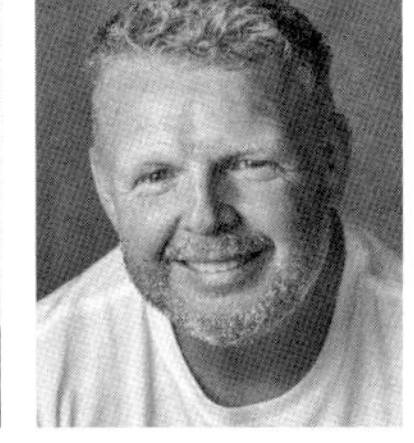

Glen
pp. 20-21

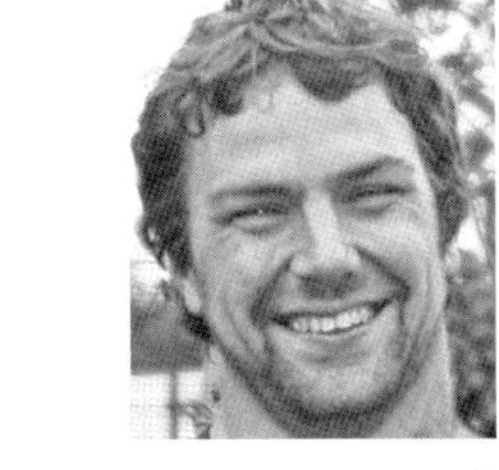
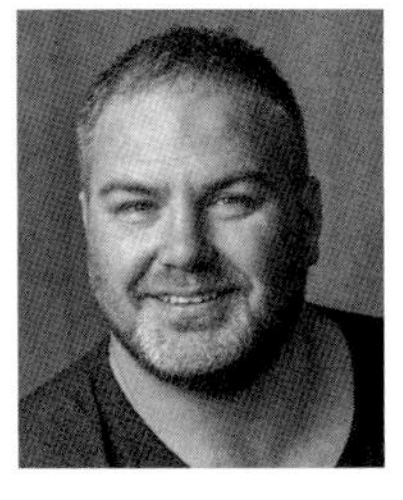

Ian
pp. 30-31

THEN & NOW

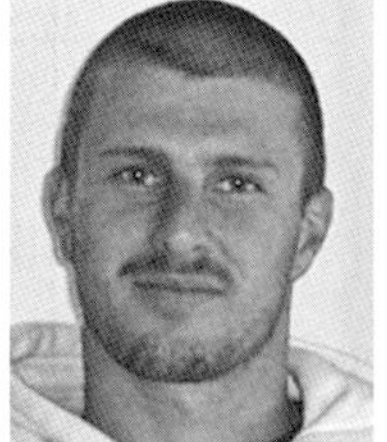

Jason
pp. 16-17

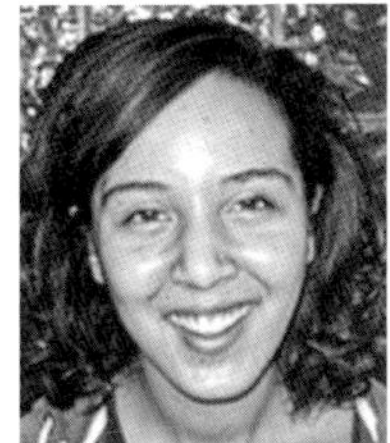

Jess
pp. 32-33

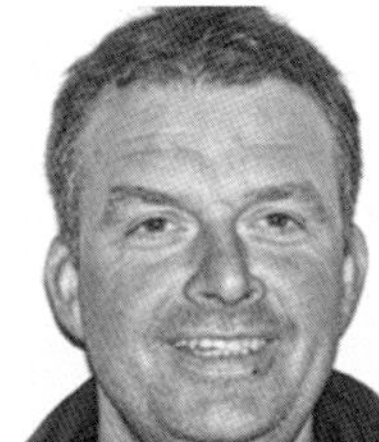

Jimmy
pp. 12-13

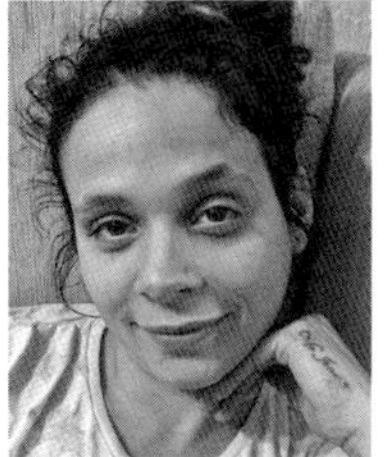
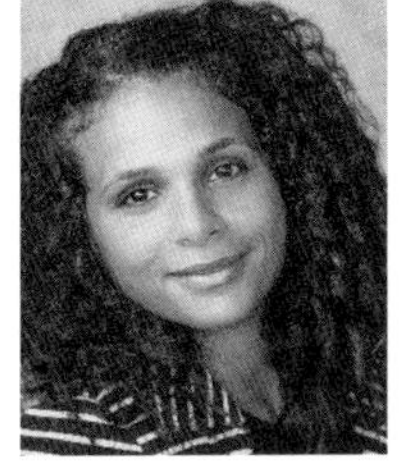
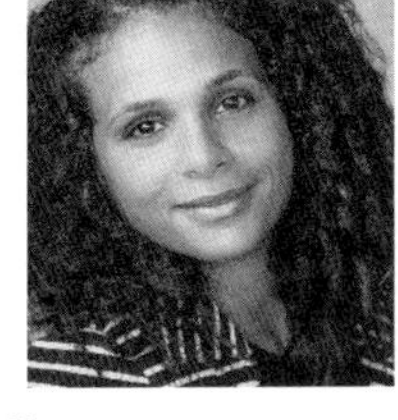
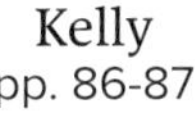

Kelly
pp. 86-87

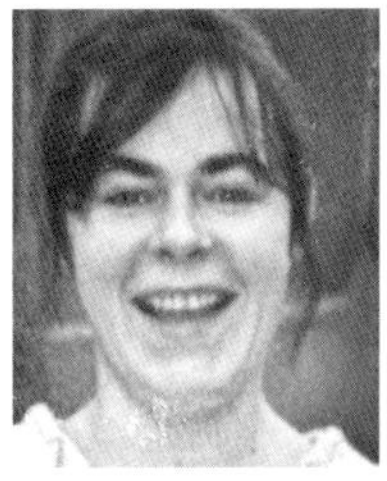
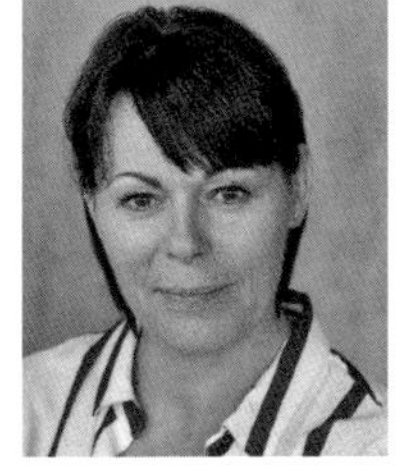
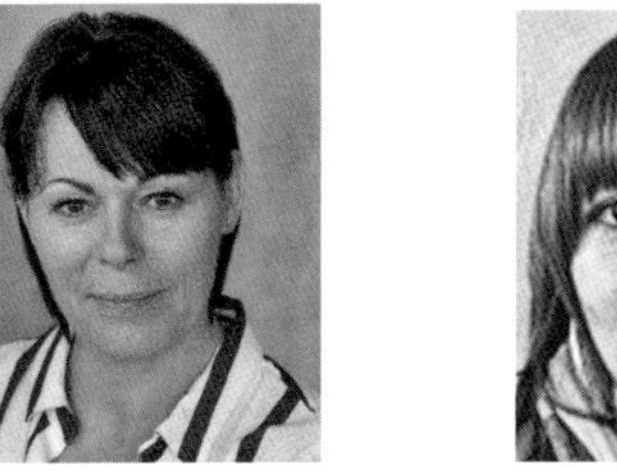
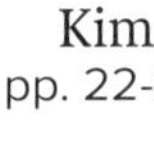

Kim
pp. 22-23

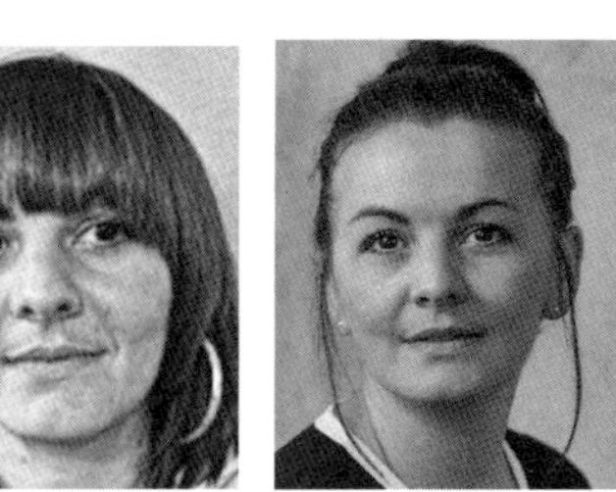

Kirsty
pp. 28-29

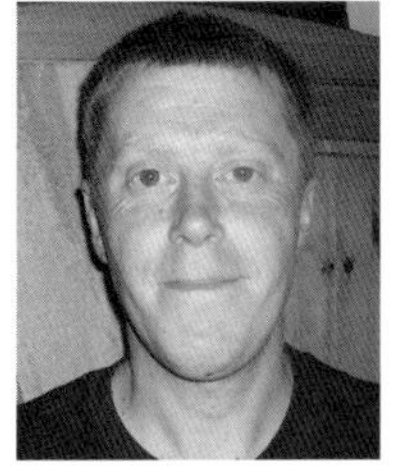
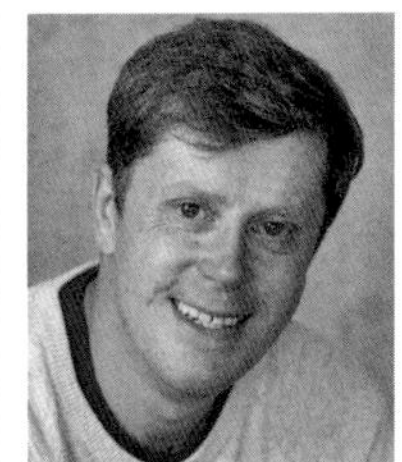

Luke
pp. 66-67

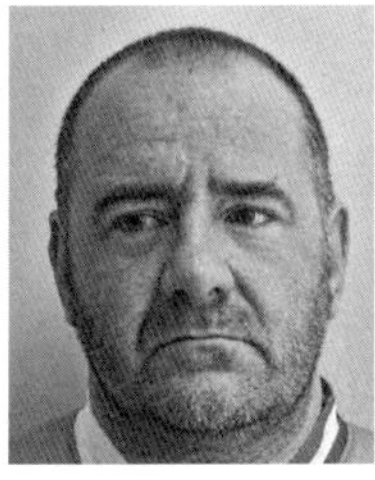
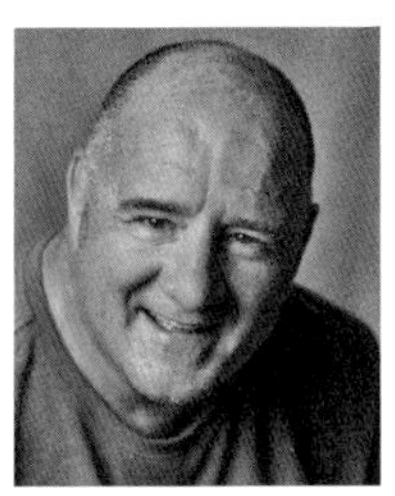

Malcolm
pp. 56-57

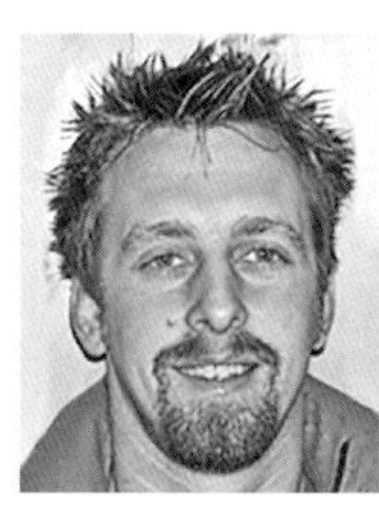
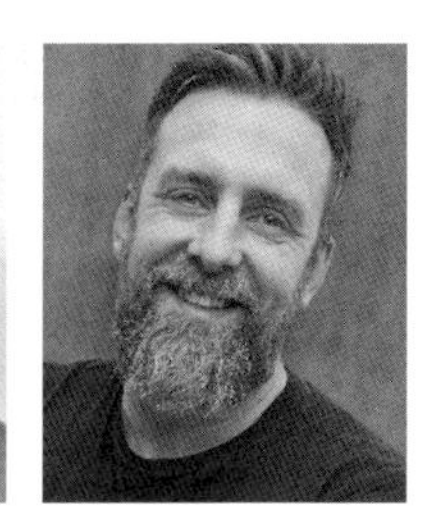

Paul T.
pp. 78-79

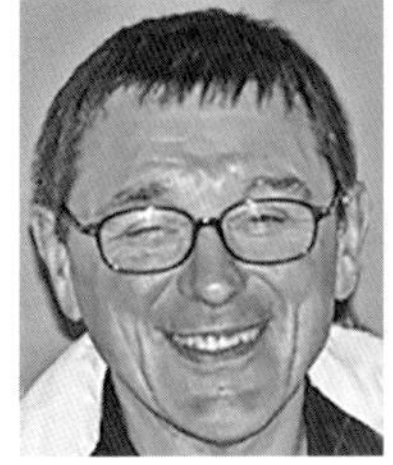
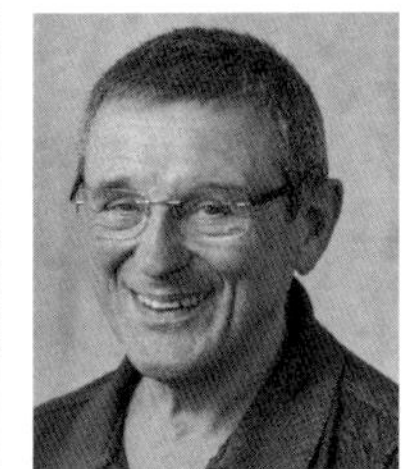

Paul W.
pp. 52-53

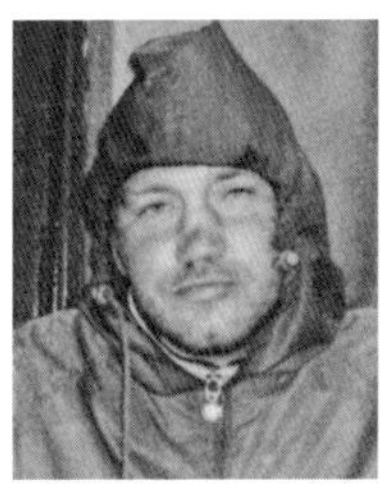
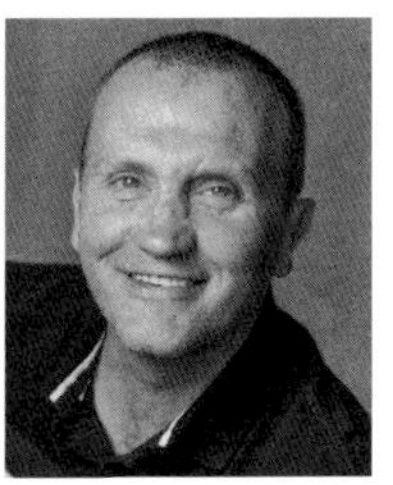

Pete
pp. 58-59

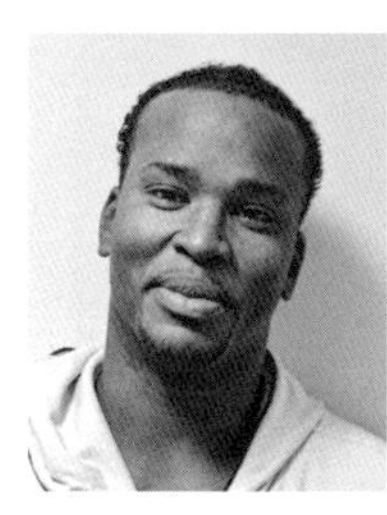
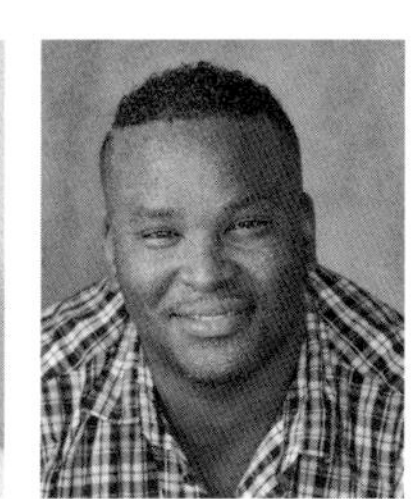

Rasool
pp. 96-97

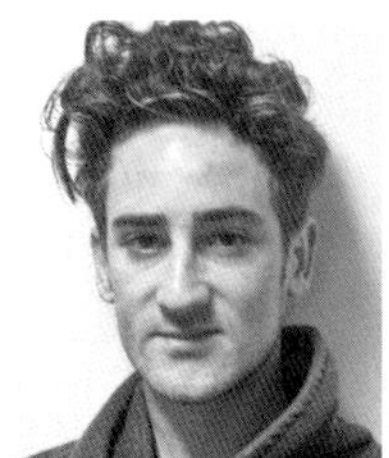
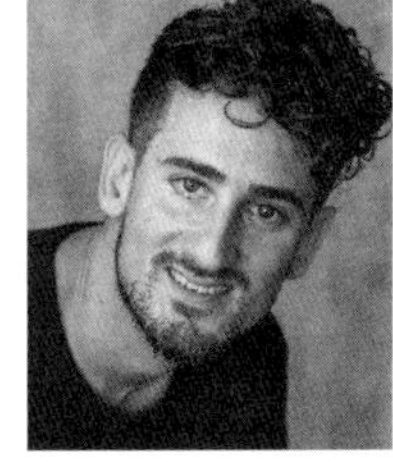
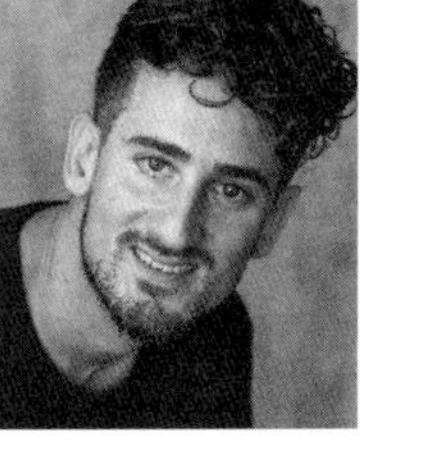

Richard
pp. 24-25

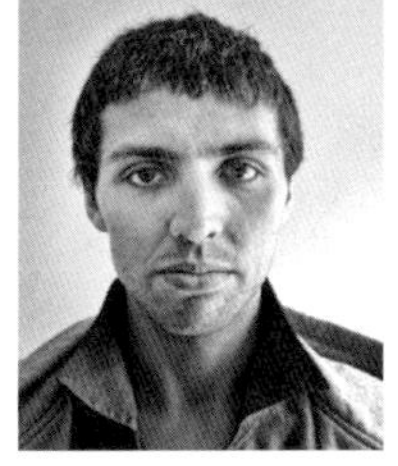
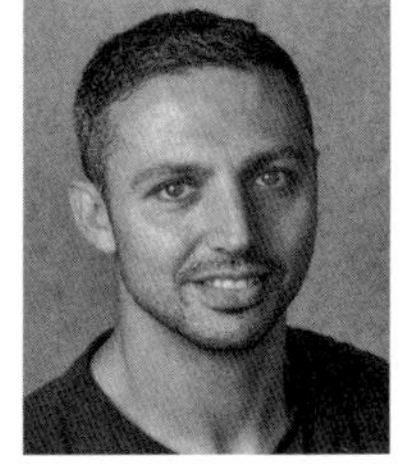

Ricky
pp. 62-63

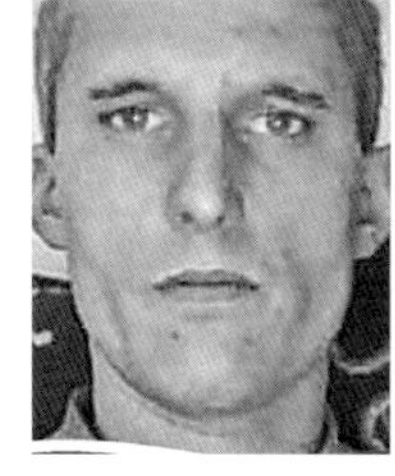
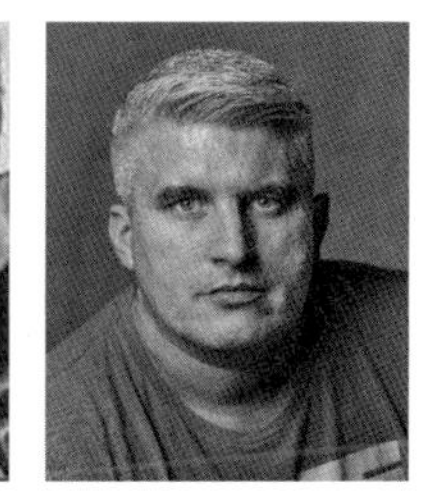

Rob
pp. 72-73

THEN & NOW

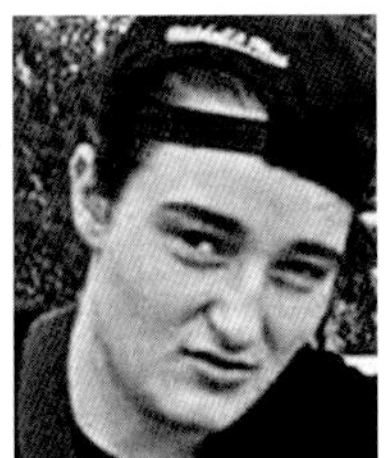

Sara
pp. 64-65

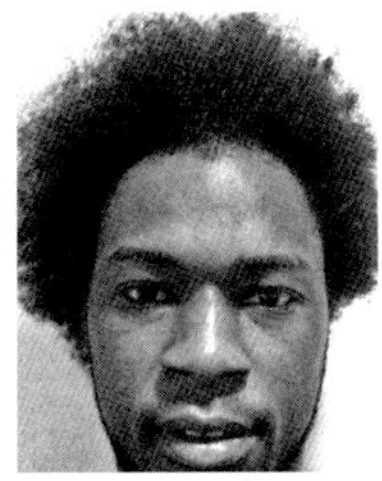

Sekou
pp. 90-91

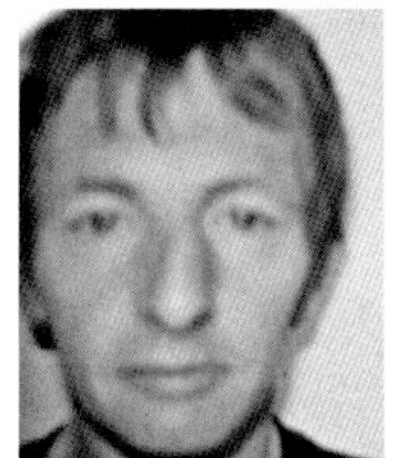

Stephen
pp. 84-85

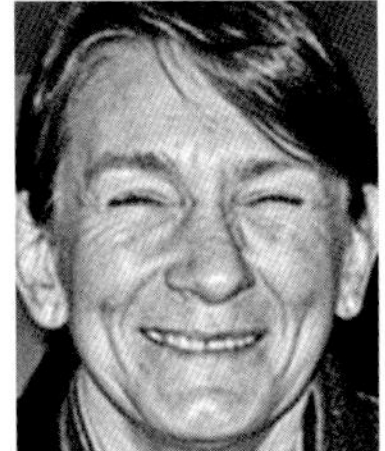
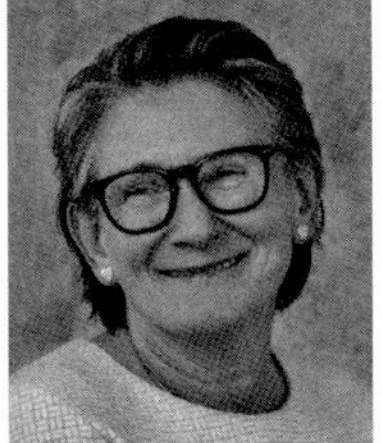
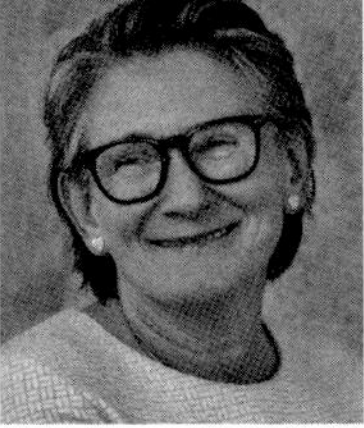

Tanya
pp. 10-11

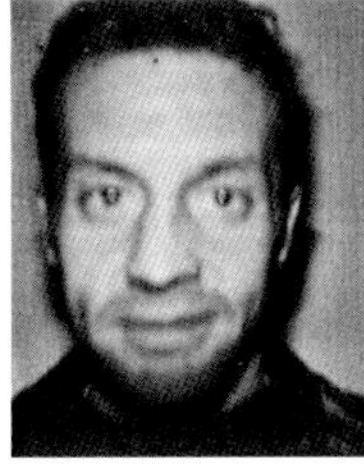
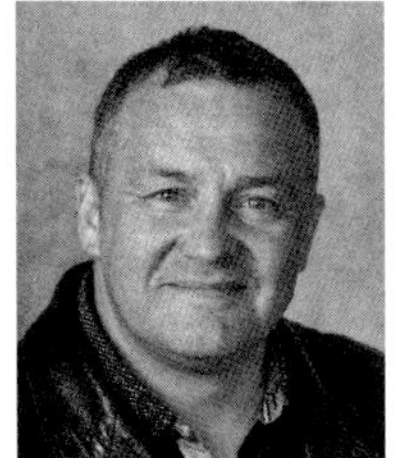

Timon
pp. 100-101

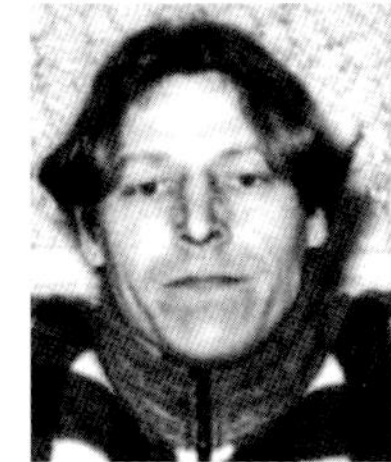
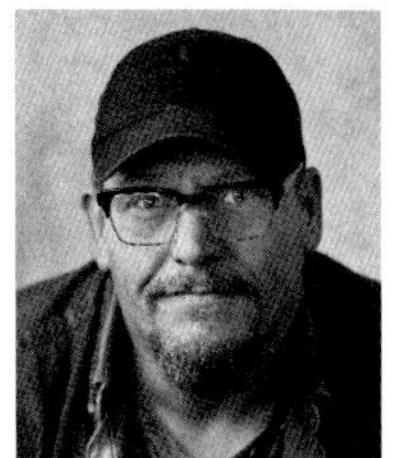

Wayne
pp. 102-103